THE HEINLE
PICTURE
DICTIONARY

HEINLE
CENGAGE Learning

Australia • Brazil • Japan • Korea • Mexico • Singapore • Spain • United Kingdom • United States

HEINLE
CENGAGE Learning

The Heinle Picture Dictionary

Publisher, Adult & Academic:
  James W. Brown

Senior Acquisitions Editor, Adult & Academic:
  Sherrise Roehr

Director of Product Development:
  Anita Raducanu

Publisher, Global ELT: Christopher Wenger

Senior Development Editor:
  Jill Korey O'Sullivan

Developmental Editor: Rebecca Klevberg

Editorial Assistants:
  Katherine Reilly, John Hicks, and
  Christine Galvin

Director of Marketing: Amy Mabley

Senior Marketing Manager, Adult ESL:
  Donna Lee Kennedy

International Marketing Manager:
  Eric Bredenberg

Production Manager: Sally Cogliano

Senior Production Editor:
  Maryellen E. Killeen

Senior Print Buyer: Mary Beth Hennebury

Photo Researcher: Melissa Goodrum

Photo Editor and Permissions Manager:
  Sheri Blaney

Indexer: Alexandra Nicherson

Project Management, Design, and
Composition: InContext Publishing
  Partners

Cover Design: InContext Publishing Partners

Cover Image: © 2004 Roy Wiemann
  c/o the ispot.com

Credits appear on page 262, which constitutes
a continuation of the copyright page.

Student Edition
ISBN-13: 978-0-8384-4400-9
ISBN-10: 0-8384-4400-8

International Student Edition
ISBN-13: 978-1-4130-0444-1
ISBN-10: 1-4130-0444-X
(Not for sale in the United States)

Heinle
25 Thomson Place
Boston, MA 02210
USA

Cengage Learning is a leading provider of customized learning solutions
with office locations around the globe, including Singapore, the United
Kingdom, Australia, Mexico, Brazil, and Japan. Locate our local office at:
international.cengage.com/region

Cengage Learning products are represented in Canada
by Nelson Education, Ltd.

Visit Heinle online at **elt.heinle.com**
Visit our corporate website at **cengage.com**

Printed in the United States of America
10 11 12   11 10 09

Contents

10 Health

11 Work

12 Earth and Space

13 Animals, Plants, and Habitats

14 School Subjects

15 The Arts

16 Recreation

Acknowledgments

The publisher would like to thank the following reviewers, consultants, and participants in focus groups:

Susan Alexandre
Trimble Technical High School
Ft. Worth, TX

Lizbeth Ascencio
Dona Ana Branch
    Community College
Las Cruces, NM

Pam S. Autrey
Central Gwinnett High School
Lawrenceville, GA

JoEllen Barnett
K.E. Taylor Elementary School
Lawrenceville, GA

Linda Boice
Elk Grove Unified School District
Sacramento, CA

Chan Bostwick
Los Angeles Unified School District
Los Angeles, CA

Diana Brady-Herndon
Napa Valley Adult School
Napa, CA

Mona Brantley
Des Moines Area
    Community College
Ankeny, Iowa

Petra Callin
Child Services Center,
    Portland Public Schools
Portland, OR

David Chávez
Horizonte Instruction and
    Training Center
Salt Lake City, UT

Kathy Connelly
Ed Shands Adult School
Oakland, CA

María de Lourdes Colín Escalona
Toluca, Mexico

Sam Cucciniello
Belmont High School
Los Angeles, CA

Jennifer Daniels
Mesa County Valley School
    District 51
Grand Junction, CO

Jeff Diuglio
Boston University CELOP /
    Harvard IELP
Auburndale, MA

Dana Dusbiber
Luther Burbank High School
Sacramento, CA

Michal Eskayo
St. Augustine College
Chicago, IL

Sara Farley
Wichita High School East
Wichita, KS

Kathleen Flynn
Glendale Community College
Glendale, CA

Utzuinic Garcés
Mexico City, Mexico

Nancy Garcia
Riverbank High School
Riverbank, CA

Gerónima Garza
Cypress-Fairbanks
    Independent School District
Houston, TX

Sally Gearhart
Santa Rosa Junior College
Santa Rosa, CA

Julie Gomez-Baker
Mesa Unified School District
Mesa, AZ

Virginia Guleff
Miramar College
Escondido, CA

Katalin Gyurindak
Mt. San Antonio College
Walnut, CA

Orin Hargraves
Westminster, MD

Iordana Iordanova
Triton College
River Grove, IL

Ocean Jones
Merced High School
Merced, CA

Gemma Kang
Wonderland
Seoul, Korea

Vicki Kaplan
Adams 12 Schools
Thornton, CO

Dale R. Keith
Miami-Dade County
    Public Schools
Miami, FL

Alyson Kleiber
Stamford Public Schools
Stamford, CT

Jean Lewis
Clark County School District
Las Vegas, NV

Virginia Lezhnev
Center for Language
    Education and Development
Washington, DC

Mabel Magarinos
Orange County Public Schools
Orlando, FL

Elizabeth Minicz
William Rainey Harper College
Palatine, IL

Dianne Mortensen
John J Pershing Intermediate
    School
Brooklyn, NY

Kathryn Nelson
Wichita High School North
Wichita, KS

Andrea O'Brien
Lawrence Adult Learning Center
Lawrence, MA

Denis O'Leary
Rio del Valle Jr. High School
Oxnard, CA

Dianne Ogden
Snow College
Ephraim, UT

Bari N. Ramirez
L.V. Stockard Middle School
Dallas, TX

Nelda Rangel
Brownsville ISD Adult Ed
Brownsville, TX

David L. Red
Fairfax County Public Schools
Falls Church, VA

Eric Rosenbaum
BEGIN Managed Programs
New York, NY

Federico Salas
North Harris College—
    Community Education
Houston, TX

Claudia Sasía Pinzón
Instituto México de Puebla AC
Puebla, Mexico

Linda Sasser
Alhambra School District
San Gabriel, CA

Laurie Shapero
Miami Dade Community College
Miami, FL

Rayna Shaunfield
College of the Mainland
Texas City, TX

Carmen Siebert-Martinez
Laredo Community College
Laredo, TX

Luciana J. Soares de Souza
Britannia Juniors
Rio de Janeiro, Brazil

Susanne Stackhouse
Language Etc.
Washington, DC

Chris Lawrence Starr
Level Creek Elementary
Sewanee, GA

Betty Stone
SCALE—Somerville Center for
    Adult Learning Experience
Somerville, MA

Charlotte Sturdy
Boston, MA

Rebecca Suarez
University of Texas
El Paso, TX

Kathy Sucher
Santa Monica College
Santa Monica, CA

The Teachers of the Harvard
    Bridge Program
Harvard Bridge to Learning
    Program
Cambridge, MA

William Vang
Sacramento City Unified
    School District
Sacramento, CA

James R. Voelkel
Dibner Institute for the History of
    Science and Technology
Cambridge, MA

Wendell Webster
Houston READ Commission
Houston, TX

Colleen Weldele
Palomar College
San Marcos, CA

To the Teacher

About The Heinle Picture Dictionary

The Heinle Picture Dictionary is an invaluable vocabulary resource for students learning the English language. It presents the most essential vocabulary for beginning to intermediate students in a unique format. In contrast to conventional picture dictionaries that illustrate target words in isolation, *The Heinle Picture Dictionary* conveys word meaning through the illustration of these words within meaningful, real-world contexts. It also offers students a multitude of opportunities to see, use, hear, and practice these words in context.

The dictionary is organized into 16 thematic units. Each two-page lesson within a unit focuses on a sub-theme of the broader unit theme. So, for example, under the unit theme of *Housing,* there are lessons focusing on different styles of houses, specific rooms of a house, finding a house, household problems, household chores, etc.

The focal point of each lesson is the word list and the corresponding illustration(s) and/or photograph(s) that illustrate the words. The word lists are arranged for ease of navigation, with the words appearing in the order in which they are illustrated in the art. Singular words in the word list are preceded by an indefinite article (or the definite article, in special cases where the definite article would be more common or appropriate). The inclusion of articles is intended to help students understand when and how articles should be used with the words in the dictionary.

Each lesson includes *Words in Context, Words in Action,* and *Word Partnerships. Words in Context* is a short reading that features a selection of the words from the word list. *Words in Action* is a pair of activities that help students put the words into meaningful use. *Word Partnerships* is a selection of collocations that exposes students to high-frequency English word pairings using words from the word list.

Scientific Research Based

The Heinle Picture Dictionary was developed with research in mind. Research supports the idea that vocabulary is most effectively learned through repeated and varied exposure (Anderson, 1999) and through a strategic approach (Taylor, Graves, van den Broek, 2000). *The Heinle Picture Dictionary* provides students with not only clear illustrations to illuminate word meaning, but also numerous opportunities to encounter and use new vocabulary. The result is an approach to vocabulary learning that reinforces understanding of word meaning and helps students take ownership of new words.

The Heinle Picture Dictionary is adaptable to a variety of situations and purposes. Appropriate for both classroom and self study, *The Heinle Picture Dictionary* can be used as a stand-alone vocabulary and language learning resource or, using the array of available ancillaries, as the core of *The Heinle Picture Dictionary* program.

Word Lists

The following list includes a few ideas that can be incorporated into the class to provide practice with the vocabulary:

- **Brainstorm to gather ideas.** With the books closed, ask students to brainstorm words they think might be in the lesson you are about to begin. Then have students check to see how many items they predicted correctly.

- **Check to see what the students already know.** As a class, ask students to cover the word lists and identify pictures by numbers.

- **Introduce vocabulary.** Present each word to the students. Ask them to listen to you or the audio and repeat. Help them with pronunciation and check for comprehension.

- **Quiz students.** Ask students to point to pictures that correspond to words you call out. *Or,* ask students to point to pictures that correspond to words embedded within a sentence or a paragraph that you read aloud.

- **Have students quiz each other.** Student A covers the word list and student B asks student A to point to the correct picture. *Or,* ask students to work in pairs to define the meaning of words in the list using their own words.

- **Play Bingo.** Ask students to choose any five words from the list and write them down on a piece of paper. Call out words to the class at random. When a student has a word on his/her list, he/she checks it off. The first student to check off every word on his/her list wins.

- **Classify.** Ask students to classify vocabulary on a chart or in a cluster diagram. Templates for many charts and diagrams are available on the *Activity Bank CD-ROM* or can be produced by the students.

- **Do a dictation.** Give students spelling tests, dictate the *Words in Context,* or dictate sentences containing vocabulary. This can also be done as a pairwork activity in which one student gives the words or sentences to another.

- **Have students create sentences/paragraphs.** Ask students to produce sentences or paragraphs using the vocabulary from the list.

- **Elicit more vocabulary.** Elicit from students additional vocabulary related to the theme of the lesson.

- **Encourage discussion.** Discuss the theme of the lesson, using the new vocabulary.

- **Provide real-life tasks.** Have students use the vocabulary in a real-life task, such as making floor plans, giving directions, giving instructions, completing forms, etc.

Words in Context

Words in Context introduces students to words from the word list in the context of a reading about the lesson topic. In addition to introducing vocabulary from the lesson in context, these readings offer a number of pedagogical possibilities.

They provide interesting information that can be used to stimulate classroom discussion. The readings can also be used for classroom dictations or as models for writing.

Words in Action

The *Words in Action* section provides students with multi-skill activities to practice and reinforce the vocabulary. These activities are especially useful as an application after the students become comfortable with the new vocabulary.

Word Partnerships

The *Word Partnerships* section provides students with common high-frequency collocations using words from the word list. It may be helpful to show pictures or bring in real-life examples of the noun and adjective-based collocations, or to "perform" verb-based collocations for the class. Many of the "Word List" activities suggested above would work equally well with *Word Partnerships*.

Teaching Grammar with *The Heinle Picture Dictionary*

The scenes in *The Heinle Picture Dictionary* can be used as an effective tool for practicing grammar tenses. The following is an approach to using the dictionary to teach grammar.

Tell students to look at a scene in one of the lessons. Identify a time frame. For example, if you're teaching present continuous, tell the students to imagine that everything in the scene is happening now.

1. Identify the context—usually a story, a class discussion, or a task can work well here. Avoid correcting students at this point.

2. Reveal the objective. Let the students know the particular grammar point you will focus upon.

3. Present the structure using a simple chart. Remember to keep the context in mind.

4. Ask students to describe the picture, using the target tense. As an additional challenge, you may have students ask each other questions about the illustration.

5. Provide either written or oral practice.

6. Evaluate students' use and comprehension of the structure.

7. Provide an application that allows students to use the structure in a more independent and less guided way.

The same scene can be used over and over again to teach different tenses. The next time the scene is used to teach or review a tense, students will already be familiar with the vocabulary, so it will be easier for them to focus on the grammar.

Supplemental Materials

The Lesson Planner. The full-color *Lesson Planner* provides complete lesson plans at three different levels for each lesson in the dictionary. The levels are coded as follows:

  ▯ = Beginning Low

  ▯ ▯ = Beginning

  ▯ ▯ ▯ = Beginning High/Intermediate Low

Classes often differ in exact level, so please consider these levels only as suggestions. They are primarily given to indicate the increasing difficulty of the lessons.

The lesson plans take the instructor through each stage of a lesson, from warm-up, introduction, and presentation through to practice and application. The *Lesson Planner* includes the *Activity Bank CD-ROM*, which has additional activities for each unit. These worksheets can be downloaded and customized by the instructor.

Each of the three lesson plans provided for every lesson in *The Heinle Picture Dictionary* is designed to be used in a full class period. This planner is different from a traditional teacher's guide in that it not only gives suggestions for what to do with the student material, but it also helps you to organize your entire class experience into a proven and productive lesson plan approach. The objective-driven lesson plans propose a variety of tasks and activities that culminate in an application and often an optional project.

As you incorporate lesson plans into your instruction, you will discover how this approach ensures effective teaching and successful language learning. The lesson plan format consists of the following:

▯ **Warm-up and Review**—Students are given tasks or activities that will activate their prior knowledge, preparing them for the lesson.

▯ **Introduction**—Students are given the objective for the lesson. This is an essential step as students must know what it is they will be learning and why they will be learning it.

▯ **Presentation**—Teachers present new material, check student understanding, and prepare students for the practice.

▯ **Practice**—Students practice an activity provided by the teacher.

▯ **Evaluation**—The teacher checks the students' ability to do the previous practice as an indication of their readiness to perform the application.

▯ **Application**—Students demonstrate their ability to perform the objective of a lesson more independently, with less teacher guidance.

The HPD Workbooks. There are two HPD Workbooks, each with its own supplemental audio program. There will be one for beginning and the other for intermediate students. The full-color workbooks are correlated page by page to the dictionary. They have a variety of activities, including listening activities, to support student learning.

The HPD Interactive CD-ROM. This interactive CD-ROM provides an abundance of interactive activities to reinforce the vocabulary learned in *The Heinle Picture Dictionary*.

The HPD Audio Tapes and CDs include the readings and word lists.

We hope *The Heinle Picture Dictionary* becomes a source of engaging, meaningful language learning for your students. Please feel free to contact us at www.heinle.com with your comments and suggestions.

Welcome to
THE HEINLE PICTURE DICTIONARY

Four thousand words are presented in 16 contextualized, thematic units. Each lesson in the unit presents vocabulary through color photographs and illustrations, contextualized readings, high-frequency word patterns study, and active learning opportunities.

"Words in Context" shows how the language is actually used through accessible, contextualized readings at a high-beginning level.

Tools and Supplies 1

Words in Context

I go to hardware stores a lot because I work in construction. I keep my **wrench**, my **hammer**, and my **screwdriver** in my **tool belt**. Those are the **tools** I use the most.

Hand Tools

Electrical

Plumbing

Power Tools

1 a utility knife	7 a file	13 a vise	19 electrical tape	25 a pipe wrench	
2 a C-clamp	8 a caulking gun	14 a chisel	20 an extension cord	26 a pipe	
3 a sledgehammer	9 a hammer	15 pliers	21 wire	27 a router	
4 a shovel	10 a wrench	16 a level	22 a lightbulb	28 a drill	
5 an ax	11 a hacksaw	17 a ruler	23 a wire stripper	29 a drill bit	
6 a handsaw	12 a tool belt	18 a screwdriver	24 (pipe) fittings	30 a blade	
				31 a circular saw	
				32 a power sander	

Word Partnerships

a tool	bench
	box
a Phillips	screwdriver
a flathead	
an electric	drill
a cordless	

Words in Action

1. Which items on the list have you used? What job did you do with each item?
2. Which tools would you use to:
   a. build a bookcase?
   b. wire a house?
   c. install a sink?

160   161

"Word Partnerships" expands students' use and understanding of high-frequency word patterns and collocations.

"Words in Action" gives critical thinking activities designed to help students put the vocabulary into meaningful use.

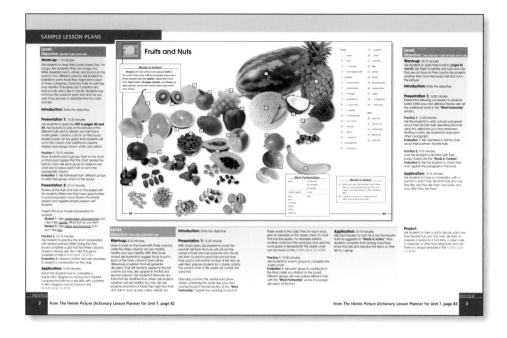

from *The Heinle Picture Dictionary Lesson Planner* for Unit 7, page 82

from *The Heinle Picture Dictionary Lesson Planner* for Unit 7, page 83

- The full-color **Lesson Planner** includes over 300 fully developed lesson plans that provide extensive support for the busy teacher.

The **Lesson Planner** provides lesson plans at three levels for each lesson in the dictionary. The lessons are coded as follows:

★ = Beginning Low

★★ = Beginning

★★★ = Beginning High/ Intermediate Low

- **The Activity Bank CD-ROM** (included with the **Lesson Planner**) contains reproducible activity masters that can be customized for individual and classroom use.

- **The Heinle Picture Dictionary Workbooks,** beginning and intermediate, emphasize vocabulary and listening skills. Each workbook has its own audio program.

- **The Heinle Picture Dictionary Interactive CD-ROM** offers additional vocabulary practice through activities, games, and word webs.

Numbers

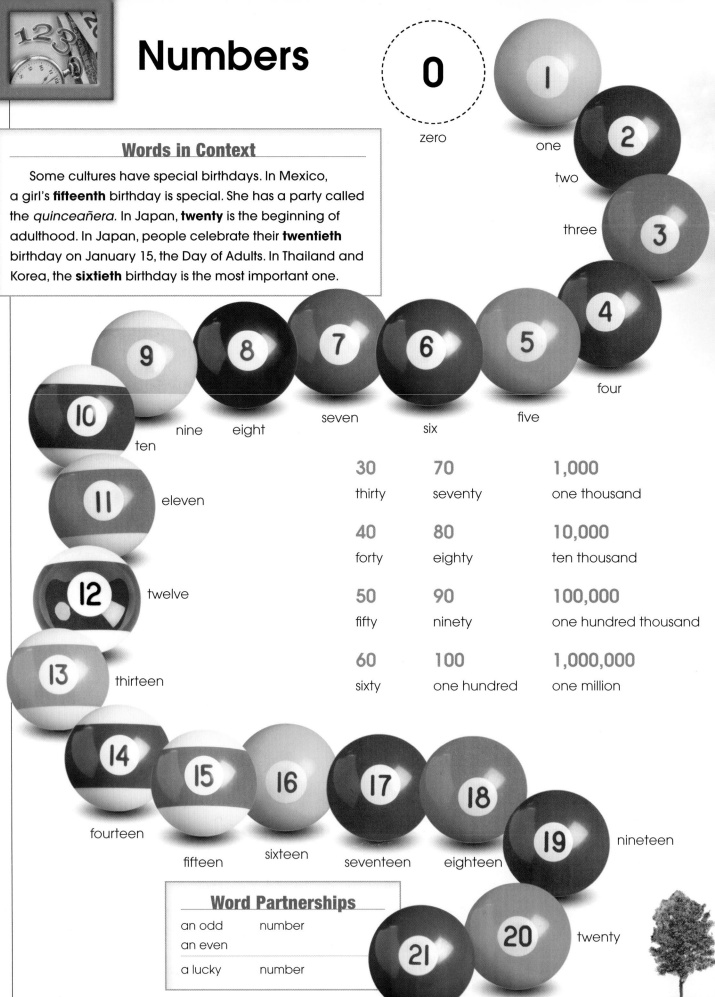

one

two

three

four

Words in Context

Some cultures have special birthdays. In Mexico, a girl's **fifteenth** birthday is special. She has a party called the *quinceañera*. In Japan, **twenty** is the beginning of adulthood. In Japan, people celebrate their **twentieth** birthday on January 15, the Day of Adults. In Thailand and Korea, the **sixtieth** birthday is the most important one.

nine   eight   seven   six   five

ten

eleven

twelve

thirteen

fourteen   fifteen   sixteen   seventeen   eighteen   nineteen

twenty

twenty-one

30 thirty	70 seventy	1,000 one thousand
40 forty	80 eighty	10,000 ten thousand
50 fifty	90 ninety	100,000 one hundred thousand
60 sixty	100 one hundred	1,000,000 one million

Word Partnerships

an odd	number
an even	
a lucky	number

2

21st	twenty-first
20th	twentieth
19th	nineteenth
18th	eighteenth
17th	seventeenth
16th	sixteenth
15th	fifteenth
14th	fourteenth
13th	thirteenth
12th	twelfth
11th	eleventh
10th	tenth
9th	ninth
8th	eighth
7th	seventh
6th	sixth
5th	fifth
4th	fourth
3rd	third
2nd	second
1st	first

Fractions

$1/4$ = one-quarter / a quarter

$1/2$ = one-half / a half

$2/3$ = two-thirds

$3/4$ = three-fourths / three quarters

Words in Action

1. Work in a group. Practice reading the following:
   - 25 minutes / 62 students / 98 pages
   - 12th birthday / 16th floor / 21st of May

2. Work with a partner. Ask and answer these questions:
   - What's your street address?
   - What's your phone number?

Time

I usually get up at about eight o'clock. But sometimes I like to get up before **dawn.** I love the quiet of the **sunrise.** About once a **month** I sleep until **noon.** On those days, there aren't enough **hours** in the day. **Night** comes much too soon.

Periods of time

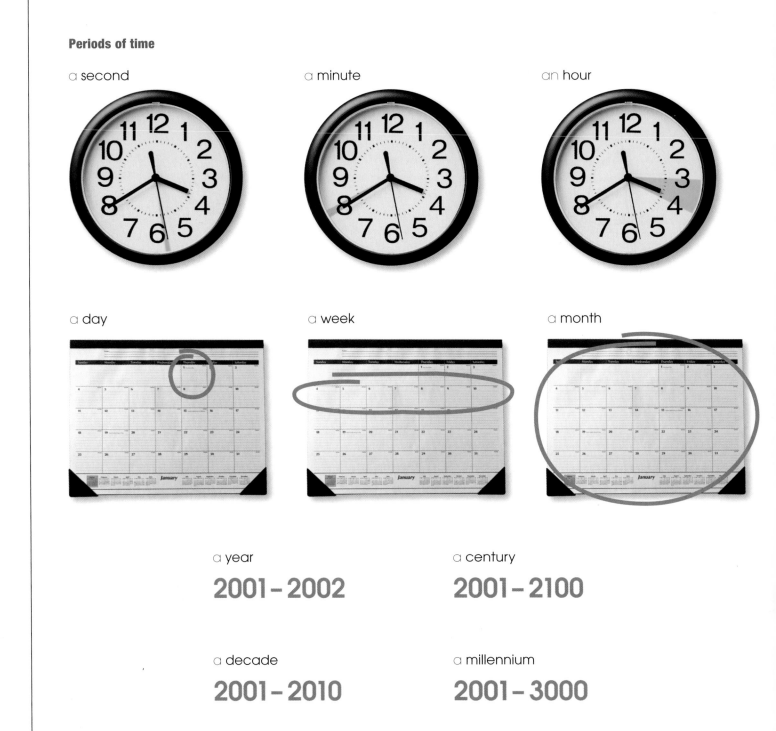

a second

a minute

an hour

a day

a week

a month

a year

2001-2002

a century

2001-2100

a decade

2001-2010

a millennium

2001-3000

Times of day

 sunrise / dawn

 morning

 noon / midday

 afternoon

 evening

 sunset / dusk

night

midnight

Clock times

 six o'clock

 six-oh-five /
five past six /
five after six

six fifteen /
(a) quarter past six /
(a) quarter after six

 six twenty-five /
twenty-five past six /
twenty-five after six

six-thirty /
half past six

 six thirty-five /
twenty-five to seven /
twenty-five of seven

 six forty-five /
(a) quarter to seven /
(a) quarter of seven

 six fifty-five /
five to seven /
five of seven

Word Partnerships	
at	ten o'clock
	night
in	the morning
	the evening
every	day
once a	week
	month
this	week
last	month
next	year
two hours	ago
five months	

Words in Action

1. What time do you usually get up? Have breakfast? Leave home in the morning? Have lunch? Go to bed?

2. What is your favorite time of day? Why? Discuss with a partner.

Calendar

1 date
2 yesterday
3 today
4 tomorrow

Days of the week

5 Monday
6 Tuesday
7 Wednesday
8 Thursday
9 Friday
10 Saturday
11 Sunday

Words in Context

The Month Poem

Thirty days has **September,**
April, June, and **November.**
All the rest have thirty-one
Except **February.**
February has twenty-eight most of the time,
But one year in four it has twenty-nine.

TUESDAY
February
1
2005

January 2005
S M T W T F S
| | | | | | | 1
2 3 4 5 6 7 8
9 10 11 12 13 14 15
16 17 18 19 20 21 22
23 24 25 26 27 28 29
30 31

February 2005
S M T W T F S
| | 1 2 3 4 5
6 7 8 9 10 11 12
13 14 15 16 17 18 19
20 21 22 23 24 25 26
27 28

March 2005
S M T W T F S
| | 1 2 3 4 5
6 7 8 9 10 11 12
13 14 15 16 17 18 19
20 21 22 23 24 25 26
27 28 29 30 31

February 2005

5	Monday	January 31
2		
6	Tuesday	February 1
3		
7	Wednesday	February 2
4		

8	Thursday	February 3
9	Friday	February 4
10	Saturday	February 5
11	Sunday	February 6

| Weekdays | Weekend |

Seasons

12 spring

13 summer

14 fall / autumn

15 winter

Months of the year

16 January

17 February

18 March

19 April

20 May

21 June

22 July

23 August

24 September

25 October

26 November

27 December

2005

16 January

S	M	T	W	T	F	S
						1
2	3	4	5	6	7	8
9	10	11	12	13	14	15
16	17	18	19	20	21	22
23	24	25	26	27	28	29
30	31					

17 February

S	M	T	W	T	F	S
		1	2	3	4	5
6	7	8	9	10	11	12
13	14	15	16	17	18	19
20	21	22	23	24	25	26
27	28					

18 March

S	M	T	W	T	F	S
		1	2	3	4	5
6	7	8	9	10	11	12
13	14	15	16	17	18	19
20	21	22	23	24	25	26
27	28	29	30	31		

19 April

S	M	T	W	T	F	S
					1	2
3	4	5	6	7	8	9
10	11	12	13	14	15	16
17	18	19	20	21	22	23
24	25	26	27	28	29	30

20 May

S	M	T	W	T	F	S
1	2	3	4	5	6	7
8	9	10	11	12	13	14
15	16	17	18	19	20	21
22	23	24	25	26	27	28
29	30	31				

21 June

S	M	T	W	T	F	S
			1	2	3	4
5	6	7	8	9	10	11
12	13	14	15	16	17	18
19	20	21	22	23	24	25
26	27	28	29	30		

22 July

S	M	T	W	T	F	S
					1	2
3	4	5	6	7	8	9
10	11	12	13	14	15	16
17	18	19	20	21	22	23
24	25	26	27	28	29	30
31						

23 August

S	M	T	W	T	F	S
	1	2	3	4	5	6
7	8	9	10	11	12	13
14	15	16	17	18	19	20
21	22	23	24	25	26	27
28	29	30	31			

24 September

S	M	T	W	T	F	S
				1	2	3
4	5	6	7	8	9	10
11	12	13	14	15	16	17
18	19	20	21	22	23	24
25	26	27	28	29	30	

25 October

S	M	T	W	T	F	S
						1
2	3	4	5	6	7	8
9	10	11	12	13	14	15
16	17	18	19	20	21	22
23	24	25	26	27	28	29
30	31					

26 November

S	M	T	W	T	F	S
		1	2	3	4	5
6	7	8	9	10	11	12
13	14	15	16	17	18	19
20	21	22	23	24	25	26
27	28	29	30			

27 December

S	M	T	W	T	F	S
				1	2	3
4	5	6	7	8	9	10
11	12	13	14	15	16	17
18	19	20	21	22	23	24
25	26	27	28	29	30	31

Words in Action

1. What's your favorite season? Month? Day? Why? Discuss with a partner.

2. What are three dates that are important to you? These can be birthdays, anniversaries, or holidays. Discuss with a partner.

Money and Shopping

Words in Context

Be a smart **shopper**! Remember these things:

- Compare the **price** of the item you want in different stores.

- You can usually **return** or **exchange** items. Be sure to keep your **receipt**.

- Try to shop when there's a **sale**. You'll **save money**!

Coins

1 a penny / one cent / 1¢

2 a nickel / five cents / 5¢

3 a dime / ten cents / 10¢

4 a quarter / twenty-five cents / 25¢

5 a half dollar / fifty cents / 50¢

Bills

6 one dollar / a one-dollar bill / $1

7 five dollars / a five-dollar bill / $5

8 ten dollars / a ten-dollar bill / $10

9 twenty dollars / a twenty-dollar bill / $20

10 fifty dollars / a fifty-dollar bill / $50

11 one hundred dollars / a one hundred-dollar bill / $100

EVERYTHING ON SALE 10% OFF [12]

29 windowshop

30 shop

31 buy

32 exchange

33 return

34 shop online

receipt
hat $27.00
tax $1.45
total $28.45 [18] [19] [20]

[21] [22] [23]

Shopping

12 a sale

13 a shopper

14 a receipt

15 a cashier

16 a price tag

17 a cash register

18 the price

19 the sales tax

20 the total

21 a bar code

22 the regular price / the full price

23 the sale price

Methods of payment

24 a traveler's check

25 a (personal) check

26 cash

27 a debit card

28 a credit card

Word Partnerships

buy things	on sale
pay by	check credit card
pay with	a check a credit card
pay (with)	cash
save spend	money

Saying prices

$1.25	=	a dollar twenty-five one twenty-five
$10.50	=	ten dollars and fifty cents ten fifty

Words in Action

1. What do you pay for with a credit card? What do you pay for with a check? What do you pay for with cash? Discuss with a partner.

2. Do you have any bills in your pocket? Which ones? Do you have any coins? Which ones?

9

Colors

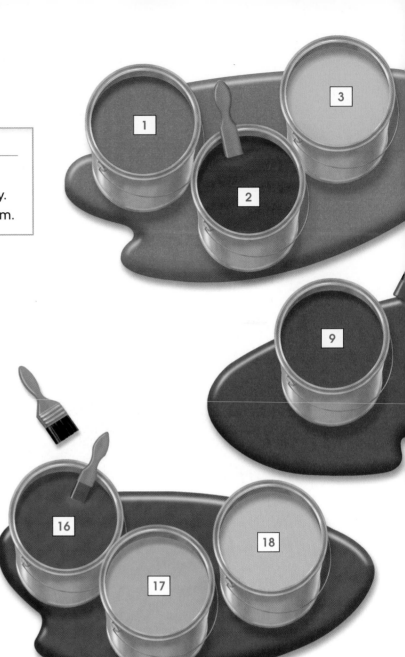

Primary colors

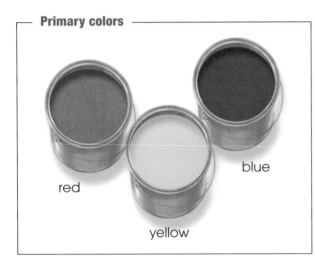

red

yellow

blue

1 red	7 lime green	13 gold	19 orange
2 maroon	8 teal	14 purple	20 white
3 coral	9 blue	15 violet	21 cream / ivory
4 pink	10 turquoise	16 brown	22 black
5 green	11 navy (blue)	17 beige / tan	23 gray
6 olive green	12 yellow	18 taupe	24 silver

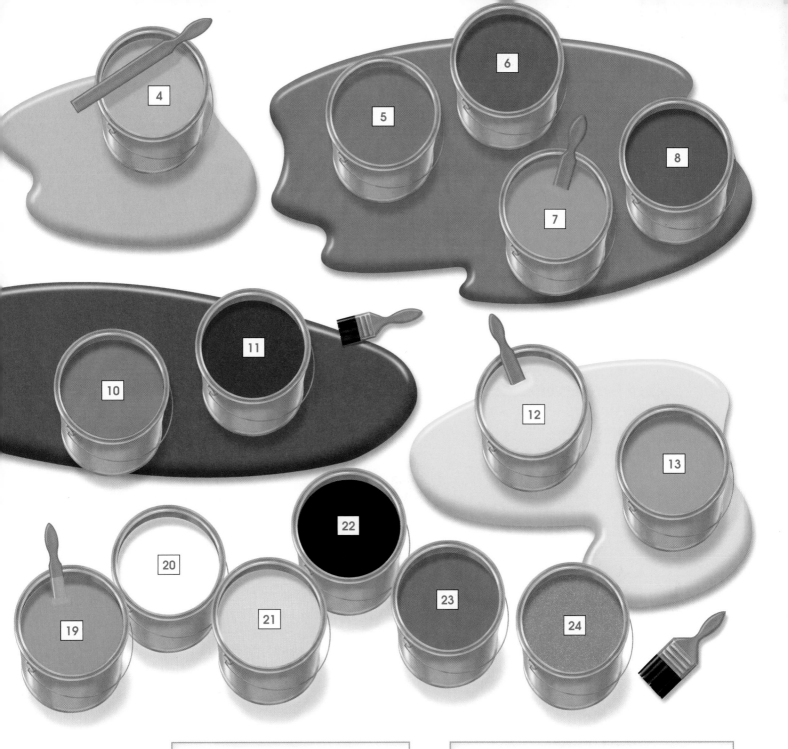

Words in Action

1. Look around the room. How many colors can you find? Make a list.

2. Work with a partner. Describe the color of one of your classmates' clothes. Your partner will guess the classmate.
   - Student A: *Someone is wearing green and blue.*
   - Student B: *It's Marcia!*

In, On, Under

Words in Context

Look around you. Can you answer these questions?

- What's **in front of** you?
- What's **behind** you?
- What do you see **above** you?
- Is there someone or something **close to** you? Who or what?

Word Partnerships

right	under
	next to
just	behind
	in front of
	to the left of
	above

1 This cat is **on top of** the shelves.

2 This cat is **far from** the other cats.

3 This cat is **on** a box.

4 This cat is **between** two boxes.

5 These kittens are **in / inside** a box.

6 This kitten is **outside (of)** the box.

7 This cat is jumping **off** the shelves.

8 This cat is **on the left of / to the left of** cat number 9.

9 This cat is **on the right of / to the right of** cat number 8.

10 This cat is **above / over** cat number 13.

11 This cat is **next to / beside** the shelves.

12 This cat has a ribbon **around** its neck.

13 This kitten is **below / under** cat number 10.

14 This kitten is **behind** the shelves.

15 This kitten is **near / close to** the shelves.

16 This kitten is **underneath** the shelves.

17 This cat is **in front of** the shelves.

Words in Action

1. Cover the list of words. Ask a partner questions like this:
    - *Where is cat number 10?*
2. Describe where things are in your classroom. Write ten sentences using ten different prepositions.

Opposites

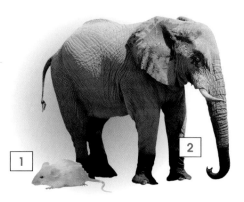

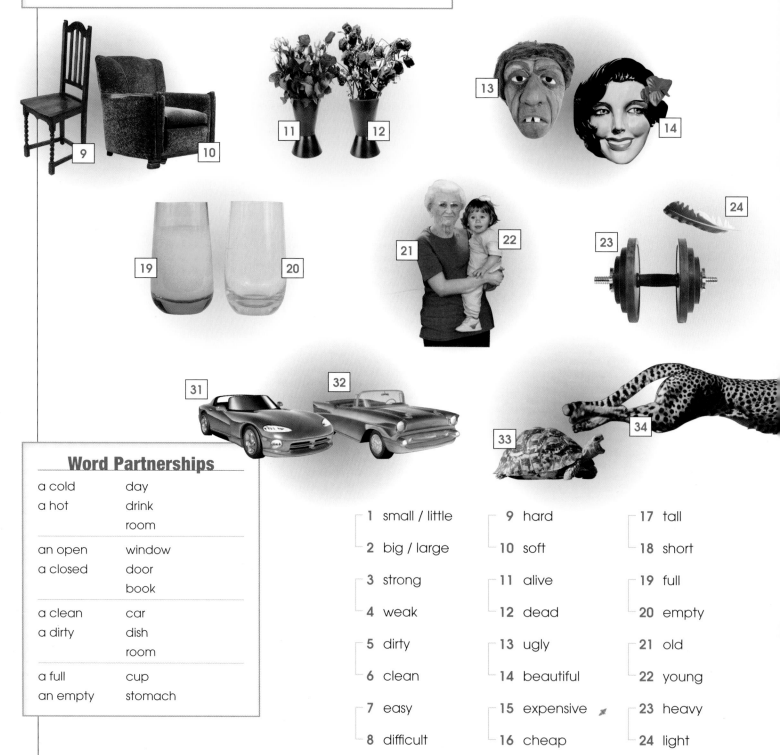

Word Partnerships

a cold	day
a hot	drink
	room
an open	window
a closed	door
	book
a clean	car
a dirty	dish
	room
a full	cup
an empty	stomach

1	small / little	9	hard	17	tall
2	big / large	10	soft	18	short
3	strong	11	alive	19	full
4	weak	12	dead	20	empty
5	dirty	13	ugly	21	old
6	clean	14	beautiful	22	young
7	easy	15	expensive	23	heavy
8	difficult	16	cheap	24	light

14

$$1 + 1 = 2$$

$$f(x) = \frac{20x}{\sqrt{x^2 + 12}}$$

25	fat / heavy	33	slow
26	thin	34	fast
27	rich	35	loud / noisy
28	poor	36	quiet
29	hot	37	open
30	cold	38	closed / shut
31	new	39	man
32	old	40	woman

Words in Action

1. Work in pairs. Say one of the words on the list. Your partner will say the opposite.

2. Describe things that are the same or different about two people you know. Use words from the list.
   - *Leo and Ali are strong.*
   - *I'm tall. My brother is short.*

The Telephone

1 a pay phone

2 a receiver

3 a calling card /
   a phone card

4 a coin

5 911 / emergency
   assistance

6 411 / information /
   directory assistance

7 a coin return

8 a telephone book /
   a phone book

9 a local call

10 a long-distance call

11 an international call

12 time zones

13 a caller

14 a phone jack

15 a cord

16 a headset

17 an operator

18 an answering machine

19 a cordless phone

20 a cell phone /
    a mobile phone

21 an antenna

22 an area code

23 a telephone number /
    a phone number

24 pick up the phone

25 dial a number

26 hear the phone ring

27 answer the phone

28 have a conversation

29 hang up the phone

Word Partnerships

make	an international call
	a long-distance call
	a local call
call	directory assistance
	911
look up	a phone number
telephone	company
	service
	bill

Words in Action

1. What is your area code and phone number?

2. How often do you make local, long-distance, and international calls? Who do you call? Why? Discuss with a partner.

Classroom

31 cheat on a test

32 fail a test

Words in Context

What does the ideal **classroom** look like? Some experts think that a classroom should look friendly. It should have comfortable **seats** and **desks.** It should have a large **bookshelf** with many **books.** It should also have bright **posters** and **bulletin boards** to show **students'** work.

Homework for Friday:
Read page 78.
Answer the questions.

Word Partnerships

go to	the board
write on	
erase	
a high school	student
a college	
an international	
a graduate	
a hard / difficult	test / exam
an easy	
a midterm	
a final	

33 study for a test

34 take a test

35 pass a test

1 the alphabet

2 a teacher

3 chalk

4 a (blackboard) eraser

5 a homework assignment

6 a (black)board

7 a bulletin board

8 a flag

9 a globe

10 a bookshelf

11 a book

12 a map

13 a clock

14 a (white)board

15 a marker

16 an overhead projector

17 a table

18 a workbook

19 a pen

20 a pencil

21 a desk

22 an eraser

23 a poster

24 a cassette player / a tape recorder

25 a student

26 a chair / a seat

27 a notebook

28 a grade

29 a test / an exam

30 a textbook

Words in Action

1. Work with a group. Make a list of everything in your classroom. Which group has the longest list?

2. Cover the word list. Find one word in the picture that starts with each of the following letters: a, b, c, d, e, f, g, h.

Listen, Read, Write

Words in Context

People learn languages in different ways. Some students like to **listen** to the language. Others like to **write** lists of words. Others like to **read** a lot or **talk** with a group and **discuss** their ideas. What about you? How do you learn languages best?

1 **raise** your hand

2 **hand in** your paper

3 **collect** the papers

4 **copy** the sentence

5 **exchange** papers

6 **write** your name

7 **read**

8 **look up** a word (in the dictionary)

9 **close** your book

10 **open** your book

11 **discuss** your ideas

12 **listen**

13 **spell** your name

14 **take a break**

15 **sit down**

16 **go** to the board

17 **erase** the board

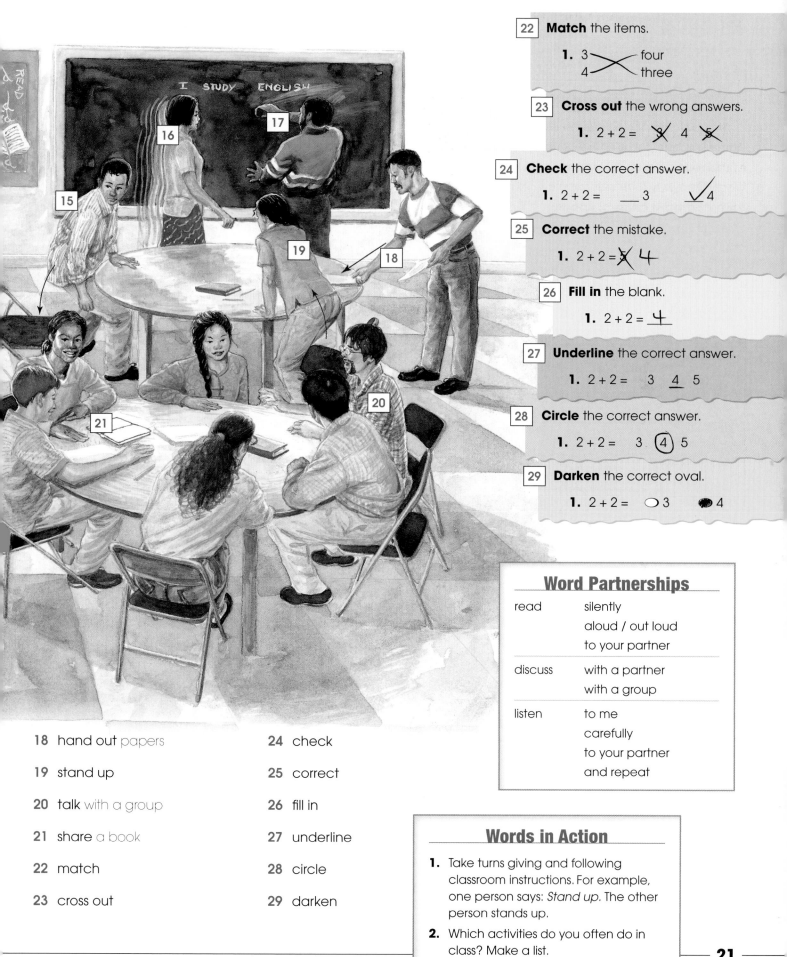

22 **Match** the items.

   1. 3 ⤫ four
       4 ⤫ three

23 **Cross out** the wrong answers.

   1. 2 + 2 = ✗ 4 ✗

24 **Check** the correct answer.

   1. 2 + 2 = ___ 3 ✓4

25 **Correct** the mistake.

   1. 2 + 2 = ✗ 4

26 **Fill in** the blank.

   1. 2 + 2 = 4

27 **Underline** the correct answer.

   1. 2 + 2 = 3 <u>4</u> 5

28 **Circle** the correct answer.

   1. 2 + 2 = 3 ④ 5

29 **Darken** the correct oval.

   1. 2 + 2 = ◯ 3 ⬤ 4

18	hand out papers	24	check
19	stand up	25	correct
20	talk with a group	26	fill in
21	share a book	27	underline
22	match	28	circle
23	cross out	29	darken

Word Partnerships

read	silently
	aloud / out loud
	to your partner
discuss	with a partner
	with a group
listen	to me
	carefully
	to your partner
	and repeat

Words in Action

1. Take turns giving and following classroom instructions. For example, one person says: *Stand up.* The other person stands up.

2. Which activities do you often do in class? Make a list.

School

Word Partnerships

elementary	school
middle	
high	
join	a team
	a club

George Washington High School
1st Semester Grade Report
To the Parents of: **James** 24

HR	SUBJECT	TEACHER	1	EXAM	2	EXAM
1	Biology	Stephens	B-	B	C+	C
2	English 2	Geofferies	A	A	A	A
3	Intro Journal	Bennett	A	A	A	A-
4	Seminar	Hurst	CR		CR	
5	Algebra 2	Jakobs	E	D	D+	C

1st Semester	Monday	Tues
8:00–9:25	25 ogy	Biol
9:25–10:20	Orchestra	His
10:20–10:40	Study Hall	Bre
10:40–11:00	Break	Study
11:00–11:55	Spanish I	Spar
11:55–12:30	Lunch	Lur
12:30–1:25	English II	Engli
1:25–2:20	Algebra	Alge

1 a coach	7 a (school) library	14 a locker	21 sports
2 a team	8 a school nurse	15 a backpack	22 Spanish club
3 a language lab	9 a teachers' lounge	16 a principal	23 drama club
4 a gym	10 a restroom / a bathroom	17 a guidance counselor	24 a report card
5 bleachers	11 a water fountain	18 an auditorium	25 a (student) schedule
6 a cafeteria	12 a school bus	19 a graduation	26 a permission slip
	13 a loudspeaker	20 a classroom	27 an absence note

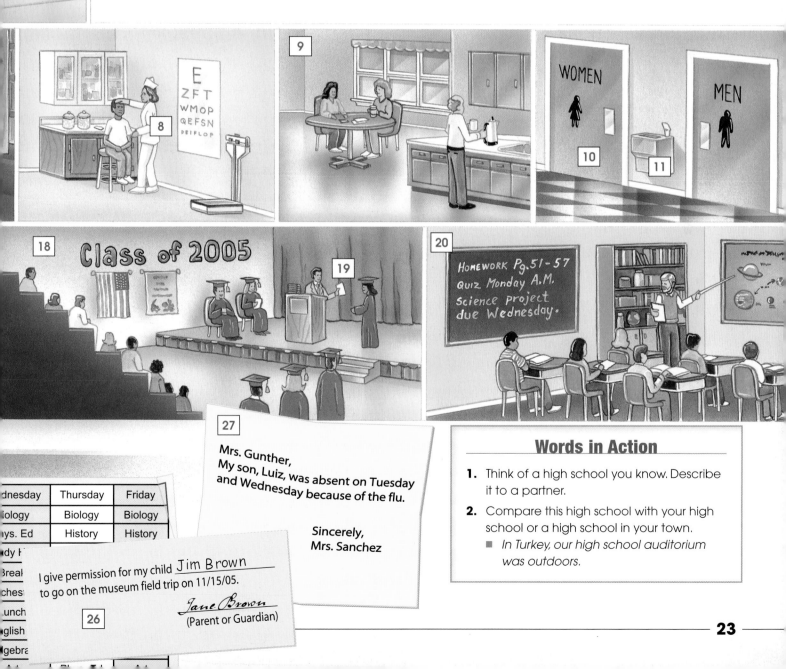

27

Mrs. Gunther,
My son, Luiz, was absent on Tuesday
and Wednesday because of the flu.

Sincerely,
Mrs. Sanchez

dnesday	Thursday	Friday
iology	Biology	Biology
ys. Ed	History	History
dy H		
Breal		
ches		
unch		
glish		
gebra		

I give permission for my child Jim Brown
to go on the museum field trip on 11/15/05.

26

Jane Brown
(Parent or Guardian)

Words in Action

1. Think of a high school you know. Describe it to a partner.

2. Compare this high school with your high school or a high school in your town.
   - *In Turkey, our high school auditorium was outdoors.*

Computers

Words in Context

Computers keep getting smaller and faster. Scientists built the first computer in the 1940s. It was the size of a large room. In the 1970s, stores began to sell **desktop computers.** Then, in the 1990s, small **laptops** appeared. Now tiny **handheld computers** are popular.

Verbs

30 be online

31 enter your password

32 select text

33 click

34 scan

35 print (out)

2005 Monthly Reports

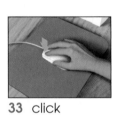

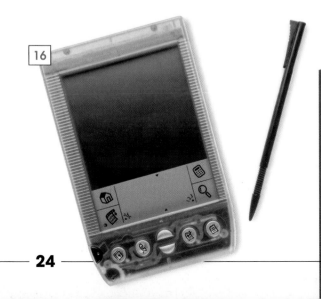

1   a CD-ROM

2   a disk

3   a window

4   a toolbar

5   a folder

6   a cursor

7   a file

8   a (drop down) menu

9   icons

10 a scroll bar

11 a cable

12 a power strip

13 a projector

14 a scanner

15 a printer

16 a PDA / a handheld (computer)

17 a desktop (computer)

18 a key

19 a monitor

20 a screen

21 a keyboard

22 an e-mail (message)

23 a laptop (computer) / a notebook (computer)

24 a trackpad / a touchpad

25 software / a (computer) program

26 a mouse pad

27 a mouse

28 a CD-ROM drive

29 the (Inter)net / the (World Wide) Web

TO: Ivan@myletter.com
CC:
FROM: fjones@messages.com
SUBJECT: HI!!

Hi Ivan,
Thanks for your e-mail.
I'll give you a call tonight.
Fred

Words in Action

1. Draw a computer. Without looking at the word list, label each part of the computer.

2. Practice reading aloud these addresses:
- president@whitehouse.gov
- http://hpd.heinle.com

Family

Words in Context

Children often look more like one **parent** than the other.
Maybe you have your **mother**'s eyes, your **father**'s hair,
your **grandmother**'s skin color, or your **grandfather**'s lips.
Who do you look like?

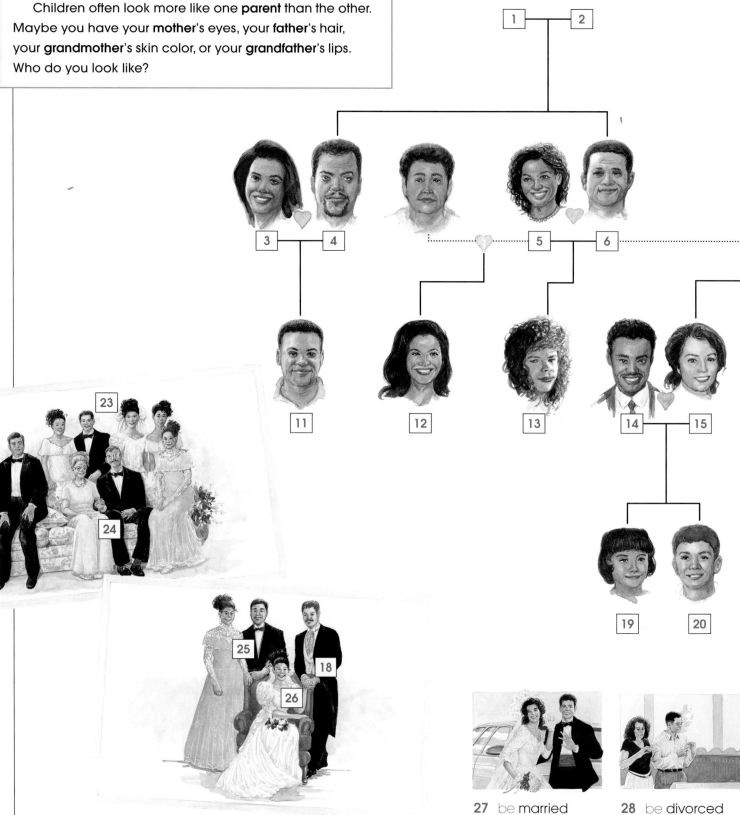

27 be married

28 be divorced

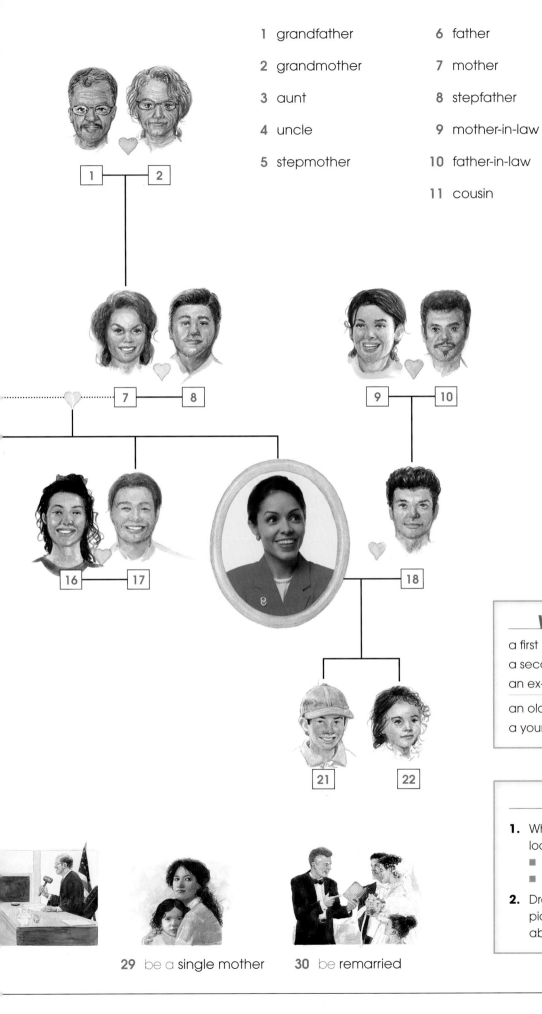

1 grandfather

2 grandmother

3 aunt

4 uncle

5 stepmother

6 father

7 mother

8 stepfather

9 mother-in-law

10 father-in-law

11 cousin

12 stepsister

13 half sister

14 brother-in-law

15 sister

16 sister-in-law

17 brother

18 husband

19 niece

20 nephew

21 son

22 daughter

23 grandchildren

24 grandparents

25 parents

26 wife

Word Partnerships

a first	wife
a second	husband
an ex-	
an older	brother
a younger	sister

Words in Action

1. Which members of your family look alike?
   - *I look like my sister.*
   - *My brother looks like my father.*
2. Draw a family tree or bring pictures to class. Tell a partner about your family.

29 be a single mother   30 be remarried

Raising a Child

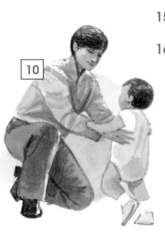

1 love him
2 nurse him
3 rock him
4 hold him
5 feed him
6 carry him
7 bathe him
8 change his diapers
9 play with him
10 pick him up
11 dress him
12 comfort him
13 discipline him
14 protect him
15 encourage him
16 help him

17 praise him
18 drop him off
19 pick him up
20 read to him
21 put him to bed

Verbs

22 crawl   23 cry

24 behave   25 misbehave

26 grow   27 grow up

Words in Action

1. Write a list of "Rules for Parents." Share your rules with the class.
   - *Parents must always protect their children.*
2. Talk with a group. What are the ten most important things to do for a child? Make a list. Put the most important things first.

Life Events

Words in Context

The Life of Princess Diana

1961
Princess Diana
is born.

1980
Diana **falls in love** with
Prince Charles.

1981
Diana and Charles
get married.

1982
Diana **has a baby,**
Prince William.

1984
Diana has another
baby, Prince Henry.

1996
Charles and Diana
get divorced.

1997
Diana **dies** in
a car accident.

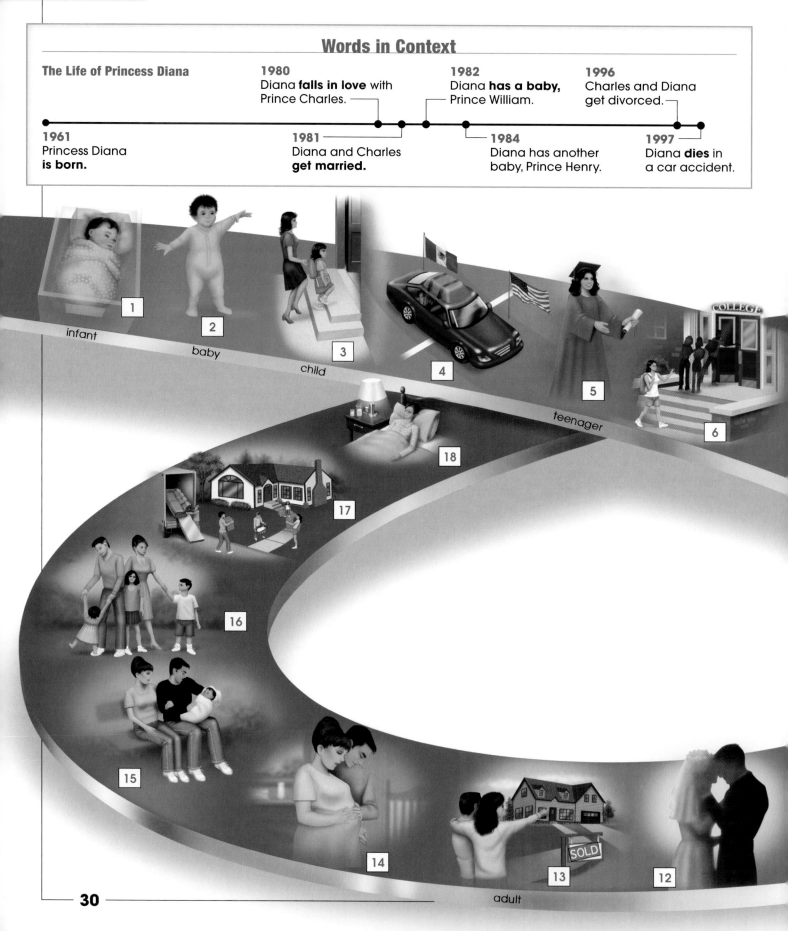

1

infant

2

baby

3

child

4

5

teenager

6

18

17

16

15

14

13

12

adult

30

1 be born	9 date	17 move
2 learn to walk	10 fall in love	18 get sick
3 start school	11 get engaged	19 take a vacation
4 immigrate	12 get married	20 celebrate a birthday
5 graduate from high school	13 buy a house	21 become a grandparent
6 go to college	14 be pregnant	22 retire
7 rent an apartment	15 have a baby	23 travel
8 get a job	16 raise a family	24 die / pass away

senior (citizen)

Word Partnerships

celebrate	a holiday
	an anniversary
	an engagement
raise	children
	a son
	a daughter

Words in Action

1. Write a time line of your own life. Use "The Life of Princess Diana" as a model.

2. What do you think are the three most important events in a life?

Face and Hair

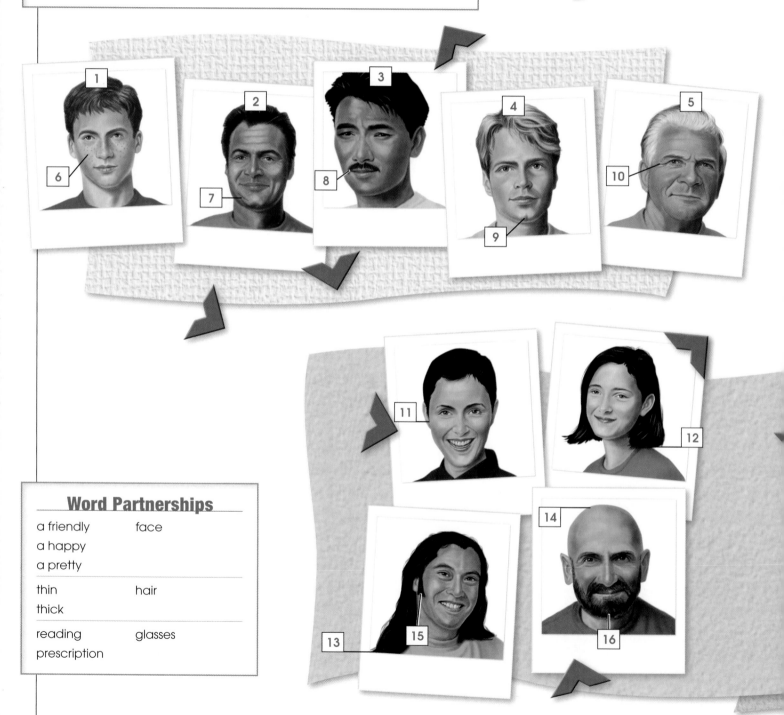

Word Partnerships

a friendly	face
a happy	
a pretty	
thin	hair
thick	
reading	glasses
prescription	

32

1 red hair

2 brown hair

3 black hair

4 blond hair

5 gray hair

6 freckles

7 a scar

8 a mustache

9 a dimple

10 a wrinkle

11 short hair

12 shoulder-length hair

13 long hair

14 bald

15 sideburns

16 a beard

17 straight hair

18 curly hair

19 wavy hair

20 pierced ears

21 braids

22 a bun

23 bangs

24 a ponytail

25 cornrows

26 pigtails

27 a mole

28 glasses

Words in Action

1. Compare yourself with a partner.
- *We both have short hair.*
- *I have freckles. Alex doesn't.*

2. Work with a partner. Take turns describing the face of someone you know. The other person will draw the face.

Daily Activities

Words in Context

José and I have two children and we both work. Our lives are busy. I usually **wake up** early. I **go** to work at 6:00 A.M. I'm a clerk at a market. José wakes the kids up and **takes** them to school. I go home at noon and **have** lunch. Then José goes to work. I **do** the housework and **make** dinner. The children **go** to bed before José returns at 10:00 P.M. The next day we **get up** and do it all again!

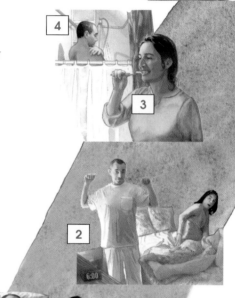

1 wake up

2 get up

3 brush your teeth

4 take a shower

5 comb your hair

6 shave

7 put on makeup

8 get dressed

9 eat breakfast / have breakfast

10 take your child to school

11 go to work

12 take a coffee break

13 eat lunch / have lunch

14 go home

15 take a nap

16 exercise / work out

17 do homework

18 make dinner

19 eat dinner / have dinner

20 take a walk

21 do housework

22 take a bath

23 go to bed

24 sleep

25 watch television

Words in Action

1. Take turns asking and answering questions about the picture.
   - Student A: *What does the family do in the morning?*
   - Student B: *They wake up, get dressed, and eat breakfast.*

2. Tell your partner about your typical morning.
   - *I wake up at 9:00. First I brush my teeth and then I take a shower.*

Walk, Jump, Run

Words in Context

I live in Los Angeles. What a busy place it is! I often **run** because I am always late. I have to **get on** the bus at 8:00 in order to arrive at work by 9:00. There is a lot of traffic. It is probably faster to **walk.** But I study English while I **ride** the bus. I am learning a lot!

1

2

3

4

5

6

7

8

9

15

16

21

22

23

24

25

26

1 fly
2 leave
3 enter / go in
4 march
5 get out (of)
6 get in
7 fall
8 slip
9 jog
10 cross
11 run
12 get on
13 walk
14 get off
15 stand up
16 sit (down)
17 follow
18 lead
19 go down
20 go up
21 crawl
22 kneel
23 squat
24 jump
25 push
26 ride
27 pull

Word Partnerships

fall	off
jump	down
	over
get in	a car
get out of	a taxi
get on	a train
get off	a bus
ride	a bicycle / a bike
	a motorcycle
	a horse
cross	the street

Words in Action

1. What five things do you do every day? Use words from the list.

2. Take turns acting out some of the verbs on the list. The other students will guess what you are doing.

37

Feelings

1 proud	6 nervous
2 happy	7 embarrassed
3 angry	8 in love
4 interested	9 full
5 calm	10 hungry

Words in Context

People cry when they feel **sad** or **homesick.** Sometimes they also cry when they are **happy, angry,** or **scared.** People laugh when they are happy. Sometimes they also laugh when they are **nervous** about something.

11 thirsty	16 homesick	20 excited	24 comfortable
12 frustrated	17 lonely	21 sad	25 uncomfortable
13 bored	18 confused	22 surprised	
14 sick / ill	19 afraid / scared	23 tired	
15 worried			

Word Partnerships

angry	about
confused	
embarrassed	
happy	
afraid	of
proud	
tired	
frustrated	by
confused	

Words in Action

1. How do you feel right now? Use one or more words from the list.

2. Find a picture of a person in a magazine or newspaper. How do you think the person feels?
   - *She is not smiling. She looks bored or angry. Maybe she is in pain.*

Wave, Greet, Smile

Words in Context

Ways to **greet** people differ from country to country. In the U.S., people often **shake hands** when they first meet. In Japan, people frequently **bow** to each other. In Chile, women often **hug** and **kiss** each other.

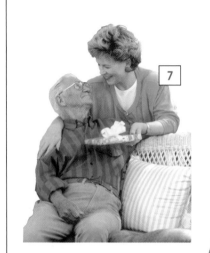

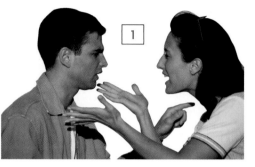

I'm sorry. 9

You look great today! 10

1 argue	9 apologize	17 hug
2 greet	10 compliment	18 smile
3 visit	11 agree	19 help
4 shake hands	12 disagree	20 wave
5 touch	13 comfort	21 kiss
6 have a conversation	14 bow	22 dance
7 give a gift	15 introduce	23 invite
8 write a letter	16 call	24 congratulate

Documents

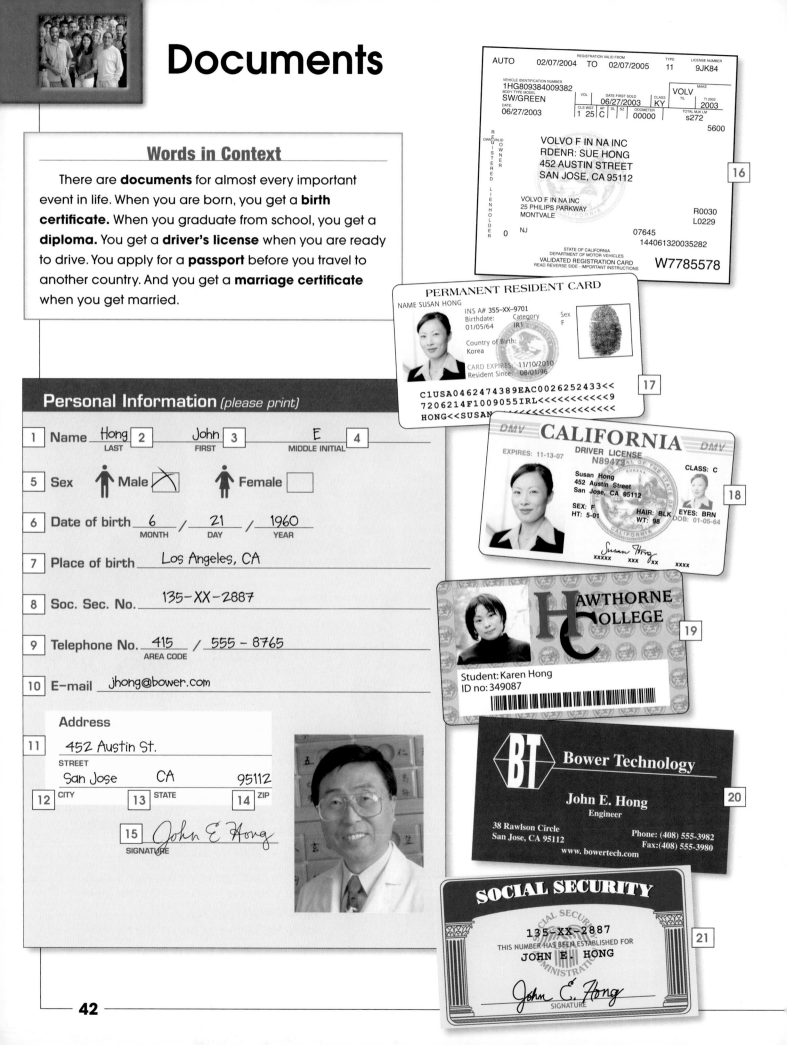

Words in Context

There are **documents** for almost every important event in life. When you are born, you get a **birth certificate.** When you graduate from school, you get a **diploma.** You get a **driver's license** when you are ready to drive. You apply for a **passport** before you travel to another country. And you get a **marriage certificate** when you get married.

Personal Information *(please print)*

1 **Name** 2 Hong 3 John 4 E
LAST | FIRST | MIDDLE INITIAL

5 **Sex** ☆ Male ✗ ☆ Female ☐

6 **Date of birth** 6 / 21 / 1960
MONTH / DAY / YEAR

7 **Place of birth** Los Angeles, CA

8 **Soc. Sec. No.** 135-XX-2887

9 **Telephone No.** 415 / 555 - 8765
AREA CODE

10 **E-mail** jhong@bower.com

Address

11 452 Austin St.
STREET

San Jose CA 95112
12 CITY 13 STATE 14 ZIP

15 *John E Hong*
SIGNATURE

AUTO 02/07/2004 TO 02/07/2005 TYPE 11 LICENSE NUMBER 9JK84
VEHICLE IDENTIFICATION NUMBER 1HG809384009382 MAKE VOLV
BODY TYPE MODEL SW/GREEN VOL DATE FIRST SOLD 06/27/2003 CLASS KY TI 2002 2003
DATE 06/27/2003 CLS WGT 1 AP 25 DL C SZ ODOMETER 00000 TOTAL MJK LM s272 5600

VOLVO F IN NA INC
RDENR: SUE HONG
452 AUSTIN STREET
SAN JOSE, CA 95112

VOLVO F IN NA INC
25 PHILIPS PARKWAY
MONTVALE
R0030
L0229

0 NJ 07645 144061320035282

STATE OF CALIFORNIA
DEPARTMENT OF MOTOR VEHICLES
VALIDATED REGISTRATION CARD
READ REVERSE SIDE - IMPORTANT INSTRUCTIONS
W7785578

16

PERMANENT RESIDENT CARD
NAME SUSAN HONG
INS A# 355-XX-9701
Birthdate: 01/05/64 Category IR1 Sex F
Country of Birth: Korea
CARD EXPIRES: 11/10/2010
Resident Since: 08/01/96

C1USA0462474389EAC0026252433<<
7206214F1009055IRL<<<<<<<<<<<9
HONG<<SUSAN

17

DMV **CALIFORNIA** DMV
EXPIRES: 11-13-07
DRIVER LICENSE
N89473
CLASS: C
Susan Hong
452 Austin Street
San Jose, CA 95112
SEX: F
HT: 5-01
HAIR: BLK
WT: 98
EYES: BRN
DOB: 01-05-64
Susan Hong
XXXXX XXX XX XXXX

18

HAWTHORNE COLLEGE
Student: Karen Hong
ID no: 349087

19

BT Bower Technology
John E. Hong
Engineer
38 Rawlson Circle
San Jose, CA 95112
Phone: (408) 555-3982
Fax: (408) 555-3980
www.bowertech.com

20

SOCIAL SECURITY
135-XX-2887
THIS NUMBER HAS BEEN ESTABLISHED FOR
JOHN E. HONG
John E. Hong
SIGNATURE

21

A (registration) form

1 name

2 last name / surname / family name

3 first name

4 middle initial

5 sex / gender

6 date of birth

7 place of birth

8 Social Security number

9 telephone number

10 e-mail address

11 street address

12 city

13 state

14 zip code

15 signature

Documents

16 a vehicle registration card

17 a Resident Alien card / a green card

18 a driver's license

19 a student ID

20 a business card

21 a Social Security card

22 a passport

23 a visa

24 a birth certificate

25 a marriage certificate

26 a Certificate of Naturalization

27 a college degree

28 a high school diploma

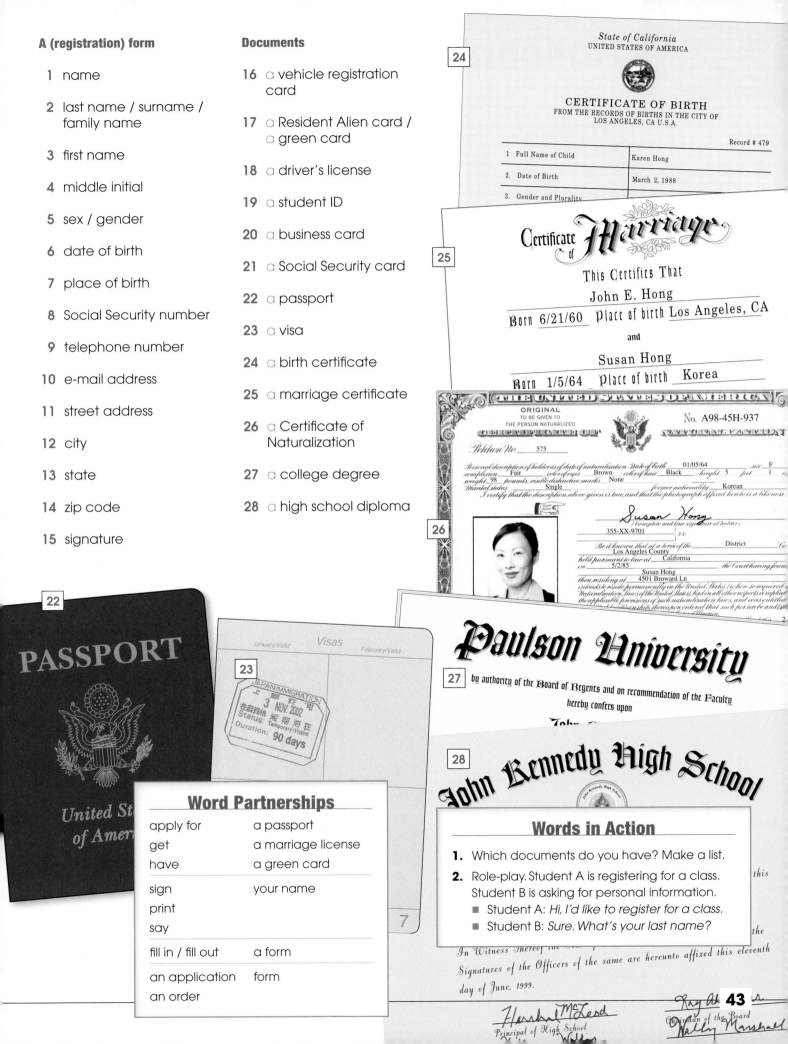

24

State of California
UNITED STATES OF AMERICA

CERTIFICATE OF BIRTH
FROM THE RECORDS OF BIRTHS IN THE CITY OF
LOS ANGELES, CA U.S.A.

Record # 479

1 Full Name of Child	Karen Hong
2. Date of Birth	March 2, 1988
3. Gender and Plurality	

25 Certificate of Marriage

This Certifies That

John E. Hong

Born 6/21/60 Place of birth Los Angeles, CA

and

Susan Hong

Born 1/5/64 Place of birth Korea

ORIGINAL
TO BE GIVEN TO
THE PERSON NATURALIZED

No. A98-45H-937

Petition No 575

Personal description of holder as of date of naturalization Date of birth 01/05/64 sex F
complexion Fair color of eyes Brown color of hair Black height 5 feet 1
weight 98 pounds, visible distinctive marks None
Marital status Single former nationality Korean
I certify that the description above given is true, and that the photograph affixed hereto is a likeness

Susan Hong
(Complete and true signature of holder)

355-XX-9701

26

Be it known, that at a term of the District Court
Los Angeles County
held pursuant to law at California
on 5/2/85
Susan Hong the Court having found
then residing at 4501 Broward Ln
intends to reside permanently in the United States (when so required

Paulson University

27 by authority of the Board of Regents and on recommendation of the Faculty

hereby confers upon

28 John Kennedy High School

22

PASSPORT

United States
of America

23 Visas

January/Valid   February/Valid

JAPAN IMMIGRATION
3 NOV. 2002
Status: Temporary Visitor
Duration: 90 days

Word Partnerships

apply for	a passport
get	a marriage license
have	a green card
sign	your name
print	
say	
fill in / fill out	a form
an application	form
an order	

Words in Action

1. Which documents do you have? Make a list.

2. Role-play. Student A is registering for a class. Student B is asking for personal information.
   - Student A: *Hi, I'd like to register for a class.*
   - Student B: *Sure. What's your last name?*

In Witness Thereof the Court
Signatures of the Officers of the same are hereunto affixed this eleventh
day of June, 1999.

Herschel McLeod
Principal of High School

Ray Marshall
Chairman of the Board
Wally Marshall

43

Nationalities

1 Canadian

2 American

3 Mexican

4 Venezuelan

5 Colombian

6 Peruvian

7 Brazilian

8 Chilean

9 Argentine / Argentinean

10 British

11 German

12 French

13 Spanish

14 Italian

15 Greek

16 Turkish

17 Iranian

18 Egyptian

19 Saudi Arabian

20 Nigerian

21 Russian

22 Indian

23 Chinese

24 Korean

25 Japanese

26 Thai

27 Vietnamese

28 Filipino

29 Malaysian

30 Australian

1 CANADA

2 UNITED STATES

3 MEXICO

4 VENEZUELA

5 COLOMBIA

6 PERU

7 BRAZIL

8 CHILE

9 ARGENTINA

10 UNITED KINGDOM

11 GERMANY

12 FRANCE

13 SPAIN

14 ITALY

15 GREECE

16 TURKEY

17 IRAN

18 EGYPT

19 SAUDI ARABIA

20 NIGERIA

21 RUSSIA

22 INDIA

23 CHINA

24 REPUBLIC OF KOREA

25 JAPAN

26 THAILAND

27 VIETNAM

28 PHILIPPINES

29 MALAYSIA

30 AUSTRALIA

Words in Action

1. With a partner, practice matching countries and nationalities. One person will say a country. The other will say the nationality. Take turns.
   - Student A: *Brazil*
   - Student B: *Brazilian*

2. Do you have classmates or friends from other countries? Make a list of their nationalities.

Places Around Town

Words in Context

I come from Concon, a small town in Chile. There's a **church,** a **gas station,** a **school,** and a soccer **stadium.** There is no **mall,** no **hospital,** no **library,** and no **movie theater.** Concon is beautiful. There are **parks** in the town and beaches nearby. Sometimes I get homesick for my little town.

1 a factory
2 a stadium
3 a mall
4 a motel
5 a mosque
6 a school
7 a synagogue
8 a hospital
9 a college
10 a police station

11 a theater
12 a movie theater
13 a church
14 a post office
15 an office building
16 a fire station
17 a city hall / a town hall
18 a library
19 a courthouse
20 a gas station

21 a parking garage
22 a high-rise (building)
23 a car dealership
24 a sidewalk
25 a corner
26 an intersection
27 a street
28 a park

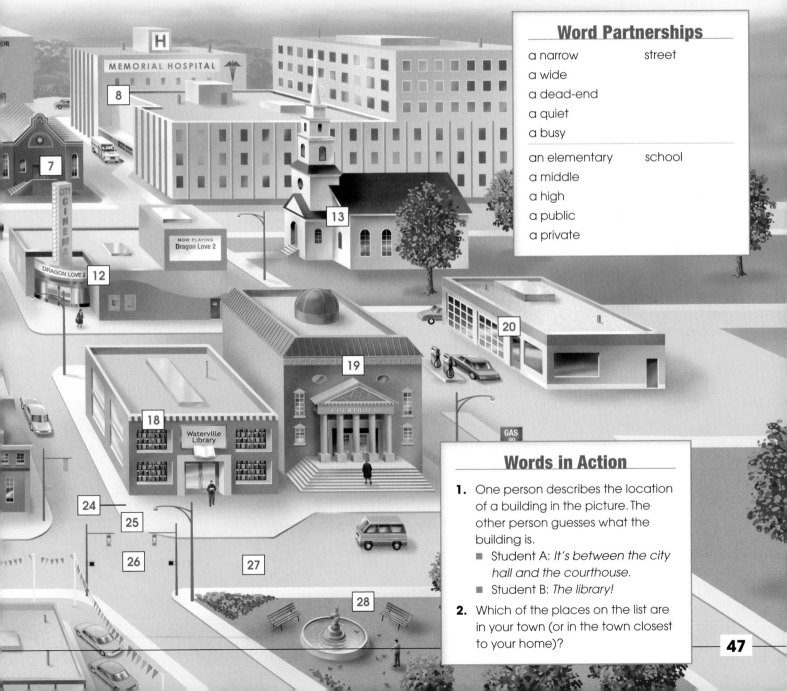

Word Partnerships

a narrow	street
a wide	
a dead-end	
a quiet	
a busy	

an elementary	school
a middle	
a high	
a public	
a private	

Words in Action

1. One person describes the location of a building in the picture. The other person guesses what the building is.
   - Student A: *It's between the city hall and the courthouse.*
   - Student B: *The library!*

2. Which of the places on the list are in your town (or in the town closest to your home)?

Shops and Stores

Words in Context

Americans shop a lot before holidays. Before Thanksgiving, **supermarkets** sell a lot of food. Just before Christmas, **department stores** and **toy stores** are crowded. Around Valentine's Day, **florists** and **jewelry stores** are very busy.

1 an electronics store

2 a clothing store

3 a shoe store

4 a gift shop

5 a jewelry store

6 a sporting goods store

7 a toy store

8 a furniture store

9 a bookstore

10 a music store

11 a hair salon / a beauty salon

12 a barbershop

13 a health club / a gym

14 a thrift shop / a second-hand store

15 a copy shop

16 a nail salon

17 a (dry) cleaner

18 a video store

19 a flower stand

20 a coffee shop

21 a pet store

22 a bakery

23 a laundromat

24 a fast food restaurant

25 a department store

26 a drugstore / a pharmacy

27 a supermarket

28 an ice cream stand

29 a photo kiosk

30 a flea market

BEST DRESS

2

GARCIA JEWELERS

5

THE HAIR PLACE

11

FRED'S BARBERSHOP

12

JIM'S GYM

13

COIN LAUNDRY

23

KING BURGER

24

Darcy's

25

FOOD CITY

CENTRAL PHARMACY

26

SALE

27

PICTURE PERFECT

29

FLEA MARKET TODAY

30

25¢

Word Partnerships

shop at	a bookstore
work at	a jewelry store
manage	a music store
own	a bakery

Words in Action

1. You need bread, dog food, aspirin, a swimsuit, and a CD. Which stores will you go to?

2. What three stores in the picture do you most like to go to? Why? Tell a partner.

Bank

Words in Context

These days many **bank customers** do not want to **wait** in a line for a **teller.** They can check their savings account and checking account **balances** by phone or on their computer. They can also **make** a **deposit** or **withdraw** money at an **ATM.**

| 1 |
| 2 |
| 3 |

| 4 |
| 5 |
| 6 |
| 7 |
| 8 |

2.5%

BANK MANAGER

| 9 |

LOAN OFFICER

Word Partnerships

a withdrawal	slip
a deposit	
write	a check
sign	
endorse	
cash	
deposit	
bounce	
earn	interest

| 10 |

C Central Bank
5001 BAY ST. BROOKLYN, NY 11235

| 11 |

CHECKING
Monthly Statement   Account 00001546093
Statement Period: 04/22/05 through 05/21/05

Page 1 of 1
Enclosures: 0

| 12 |

n Brown
Parker St.
oklyn, NY 11235

g Balance:	$552.32	Deposits/Cre
alance:	$552.32	Interest Paid
Balance:	$552.32	Checks/Debi

scription | Deposits

GINNING BALANCE
05/21   ENDING BALANCE

John Brown   712
63 Parker Street   12-3/456
Brooklyn, NY 11235 | 13 | Date _____ $ _____

Pay to the
order of _____ Dollars

CENTRAL BANK

For _____
⑈123456789⑈   001122333ⁱ 9876

IF YOU HAVE ANY QUESTIONS
VISIT ANY BRANCH OFFICE
TO REPORT A LOST OR STOLE

50

1 a safe-deposit box /
   a safety-deposit box

2 a security guard

3 a vault

4 a teller

5 a teller window

6 cash / money

7 a customer

8 a bank manager

9 a loan officer

10 a (monthly) statement

11 a checking account
    number

12 a checkbook

13 a check

14 a (savings account)
    passbook

15 interest

16 a deposit

17 a withdrawal

18 a balance

19 a money order

20 an ATM

21 a drive-up window

22 an ATM card /
    a bankcard

Verbs

23 wait in line

24 insert your
    ATM card

25 enter your
    PIN

26 withdraw
    cash

27 make a
    deposit

28 remove
    your card

SAVINGS ACCOUNT

TE	% INTEREST	+DEPOSITS	– WITHDRAWALS	BALANCE
pen account		$500.00		$500.00
extbooks			$75.00	$425.00
nterest	$3.21			$428.21
rthday gift from Mom		$25.00		$453.21
nterest	$3.68			$456.99

Words in Action

1. When was the last time you went to the
   bank? What did you do there? What
   part of the bank did you go to? Who did
   you speak to?

2. Work with a partner. One person says
   the steps to using an ATM. The other acts
   out the steps.

51

Post Office

Do you want the **mail** you **send** to arrive safely and on time? Be sure to use a **zip code** on every **letter** and **package.** Also be sure to use a **return address.** A **postal clerk** can **weigh** your mail so you will know how much **postage** to put on it.

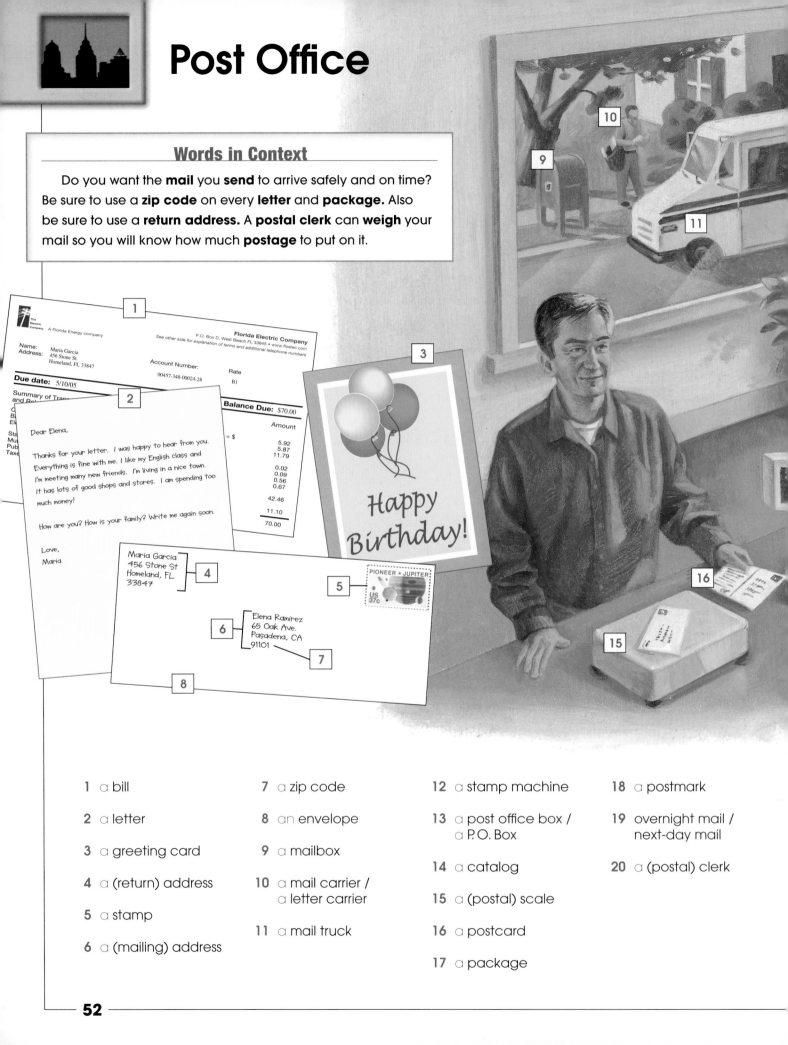

1 a bill

2 a letter

3 a greeting card

4 a (return) address

5 a stamp

6 a (mailing) address

7 a zip code

8 an envelope

9 a mailbox

10 a mail carrier / a letter carrier

11 a mail truck

12 a stamp machine

13 a post office box / a P.O. Box

14 a catalog

15 a (postal) scale

16 a postcard

17 a package

18 a postmark

19 overnight mail / next-day mail

20 a (postal) clerk

Tomorrow.

Verbs

21 address

22 weigh

23 put a stamp on

24 mail / send

Word Partnerships	
a business	letter
a personal	
a love	
a first class	stamp
a book of	stamps
a sheet of	
a roll of	
a postage-paid	envelope
a self-addressed stamped	

Words in Action

1. What kinds of mail do you send? What kinds do you get? What is your favorite kind of mail to receive? What is your least favorite? Discuss with a group.

2. Describe your last visit to the post office. What did you do? Who did you talk to? What did you see? Tell your partner.

53

Library

Verbs

26 look for a book

27 check out books

Words in Context

Libraries can change people's lives. In 1953, **author** Frank McCourt arrived in New York City from Ireland. One day a man told Frank to go to a library. So Frank did. He got a **library card, checked out** a **book,** and fell in love with reading. All of the reading he did at the library helped Frank McCourt become a successful **writer.** Now people can read his **autobiography** in 30 different languages!

Reading Room

Reference Desk

Title War and Peace
Author Tolstoy **6**

Big Book of Cheer
by Mike Nichols

Chinese Cooking

Observer
FIRE
BURNS FOREST

WAR & PEACE

Leo Tolstoy

28 read   **29** return books

1 the periodical section

2 a magazine

3 a microfilm machine

4 the reading room

5 the reference desk

6 an online catalog / a computerized catalog

7 the fiction section

8 the nonfiction section

9 a dictionary

10 an encyclopedia

11 a librarian

12 a library card

13 a hardcover (book)

14 a paperback (book)

15 an atlas

16 the circulation desk / the checkout desk

17 a newspaper

18 a headline

19 a title

20 a novel

21 an author / a writer

22 a cookbook

23 a biography

24 an autobiography

25 a picture book

Fiction 7

Nonfiction 8

Reference

9 10

Children's Section 25

Gandhi's Life 23 By Jane Smith

My Life by Abraham Lincoln 24

Fishy, Fish, Fish...

Word Partnerships

a library	book
a good	book
a boring	writer
a detective	novel
a romance	
a science-fiction	
a historical	

Words in Action

1. Imagine you will spend an afternoon in this library. What will you do?

2. Discuss the following questions with a group:
- What is your favorite book?
- What is your favorite magazine?
- What is your favorite newspaper?

Daycare Center

Words in Context

Parents should look for the following things at a **daycare center:**

- Are the children busy and happy?
- Do the **childcare workers** take good care of the children?
- Is there a special room for **newborns**?
- Are the **high chairs, potty chairs,** and **changing tables** clean?

Word Partnerships

a cute	baby
a newborn	
baby	food
a clean	diaper
a dirty	
change	a diaper
play with	toys
put away	
share	

31 a newborn

32 an infant / a baby

33 a toddler

34 a preschooler

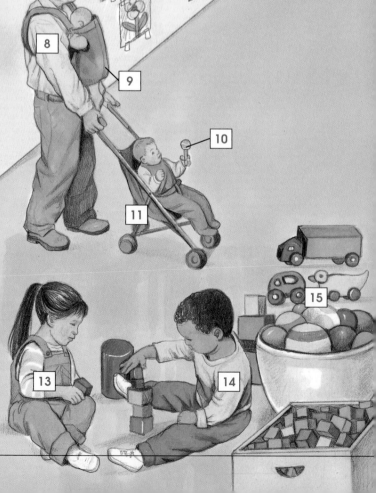

1 a nipple
2 a bottle
3 a crib
4 a playpen
5 a rest mat
6 a baby swing
7 a teething ring

8 a parent
9 a baby carrier
10 a rattle
11 a stroller
12 a cubby
13 a girl
14 a boy
15 toys

16 a bib
17 a childcare worker
18 a high chair
19 formula
20 a potty chair
21 a diaper pail
22 (baby) powder
23 (baby) lotion

24 (baby) wipes
25 a pacifier
26 a changing table
27 a (disposable) diaper
28 training pants
29 a (cloth) diaper
30 a diaper pin

Words in Action

1. Which are the 10 most important items for a newborn? Discuss and make a list with a group.

2. Imagine you have a one-year-old baby. You are taking a trip on an airplane. Which items will you take?

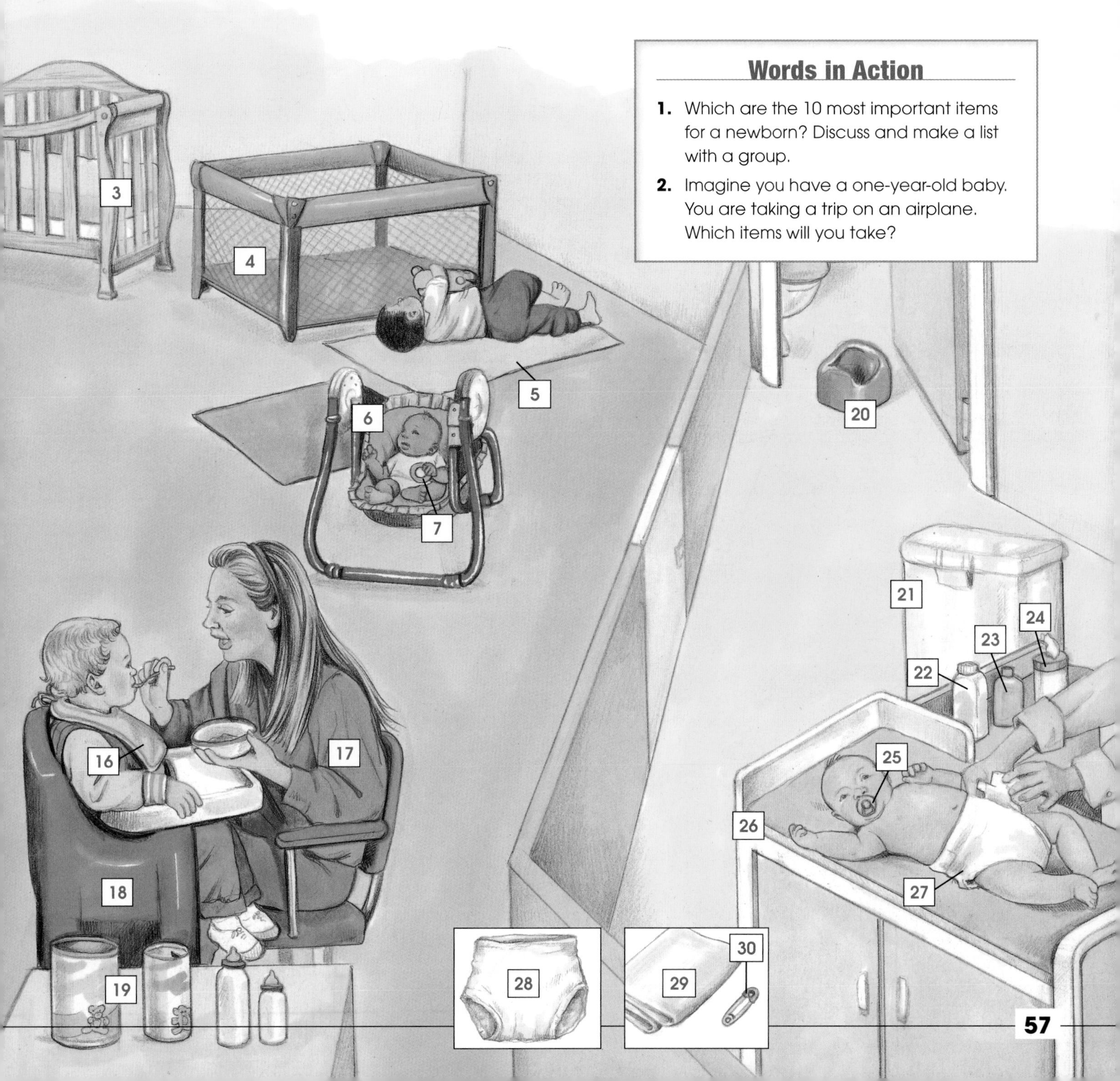

City Square

Words in Context

Prague and Marrakesh have interesting **city squares**. The squares have outdoor **cafés, street vendors, street musicians,** and **pedestrians**. There are many **hotels, museums,** and **restaurants**. At night, there are plenty of **tourists** in the squares.

HOTEL

Central Square Hotel

TAXI

Freeman Art Gallery

METRO BANK

ATM

HANDICAPPED PARKING

STOP

STOP

1. a hotel
2. a bank
3. an art gallery
4. a streetlight
5. a traffic accident

6. a (traffic) cop
7. a fountain
8. a café
9. a billboard
10. a monument

11. a (fire) hydrant
12. a street vendor
13. a travel agency
14. a handicapped parking space
15. a curb

16. a sidewalk
17. a pedestrian
18. a crosswalk
19. a sign
20. a (parking) meter

21 a tourist information booth

22 a street musician

23 a statue

24 a museum

25 a newsstand

Word Partnerships

an art	museum
a science	
a natural history	
a street	sign
a neon	
a sidewalk	café
an outdoor	

Words in Action

1. Imagine you are a tourist in this city square. Where will you go? What will you do?

2. Think about the town or city you live in or near. Make a list of all the things you can find there.

Crime and Justice

Words in Context

Iceland has very little **crime.** There are only four **prisons,** and many of the **prisoners** are part-time! There are usually only one or two **murders** a year, and crimes like **armed robbery** are extremely rare. There are sometimes **muggings** in the capital city of Reykjavík, but Iceland is still one of the safest countries in the world.

1 auto theft

2 bribery

3 burglary

4 theft

5 drug dealing

6 drunk driving

7 arson

8 graffiti

9 mugging

10 murder

11 shoplifting

12 vandalism

13 gang violence

14 armed robbery

15 an arrest

16 a victim

17 a witness

18 a criminal

19 handcuffs

20 a police officer

21 a trial

22 a jury

23 a judge

24 a lawyer /
an attorney

25 a courtroom

26 a jail / a prison

27 a prisoner

Word Partnerships

a fair	trial
a speedy	
commit	a crime
witness	
report	
go to	prison
spend time in	
get out of	

Words in Action

1. Talk with a group. Which crimes are most common in your community?

2. Put the crimes in a list from the least serious crime to the most serious crime. Discuss your list with a partner.

Types of Homes

Words in Context

Do you live in a **house,** an **apartment,** or a **condo?** There are many other kinds of homes, too. For example, some people in the Sahara Desert live in **tents.** Some people in the U.S. live in **mobile homes.** And some people near the North Pole live in **igloos.**

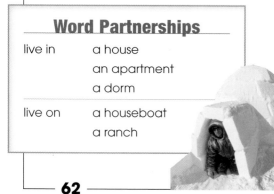

Word Partnerships

live in	a house
	an apartment
	a dorm
live on	a houseboat
	a ranch

1 a house

2 a tent

3 a cottage

4 a (log) cabin

5 a chalet

6 a duplex / a two-family house

7 a mobile home

8 a farmhouse

9 an apartment

10 a condominium / a condo

11 a villa

12 a townhouse

13 a houseboat

14 a palace

15 an igloo

16 a ranch

17 a retirement home

18 a dormitory / a dorm

19 a castle

20 the city / an urban area

21 the suburbs

22 a small town

23 the country / a rural area

Words in Action

1. What kinds of homes have you lived in or stayed in? Tell your class.

2. You can stay in three of these homes. Which three will you choose? Why?

Finding a Place to Live

Words in Context

Are you **looking for** an apartment? It isn't always easy. Read the classified ads in newspapers and talk to your friends. **Make** appointments to see a lot of apartments. Before you **sign** a lease, talk to the landlord. **Ask** questions like these:

- How much is the security deposit?
- When is the rent due?
- When can I **move in**?

Renting an Apartment

1 **look for** an apartment

2 **make** an appointment
   (with the landlord)

3 **meet** the landlord

4 **see** the apartment

5 **ask** questions

6 **sign** the lease

7 **pay** a security deposit

8 **get** the key

9 **pack**

10 **load** a van or truck

11 **unpack**

12 **arrange** the furniture

13 **decorate** the apartment

14 **pay** the rent

15 **meet** the neighbors

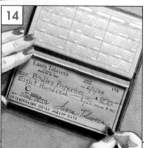

Buying a House

16 **call** a realtor

17 **look at** houses

18 **make** a decision

19 **make** an offer

20 **negotiate** the price

21 **inspect** the house

22 **apply for** a loan

23 **make** a down payment

24 **sign** the loan documents

25 **move in**

26 **make** the (house) payment

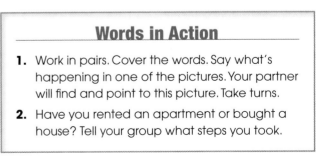

Word Partnerships

look for	an apartment	in the classified ads
		online
		with a realtor
pay	the rent	early
		late
		on time

Words in Action

1. Work in pairs. Cover the words. Say what's happening in one of the pictures. Your partner will find and point to this picture. Take turns.

2. Have you rented an apartment or bought a house? Tell your group what steps you took.

Apartment Building

Words in Context

I'm the **superintendent** of an **apartment building** in Los Angeles. We have 30 **unfurnished apartments.** Most of these are **studios.** We have a **laundry room** in the **basement.** There's no **doorman,** but I watch everyone who comes in the **lobby.** I take good care of my building.

1
2
3
4
5
6
7
8
9
10
11
12
13
14
15
16
17
18
19
20

1 a storage space

2 a dumpster

3 a superintendent / a super

4 stairs

5 a furnace

6 a water heater

7 a basement

8 a parking space

9 a studio (apartment)

10 a tenant

11 a roommate

12 a hallway

13 a one-bedroom apartment

14 an air conditioner

15 a workout room / a gym

16 a balcony

17 a courtyard

18 a laundry room

19 a fire escape

20 an unfurnished apartment

21 a furnished apartment

22 a lobby

23 an elevator

24 a revolving door

25 a doorman

26 a peephole

27 a door chain

28 a dead-bolt (lock)

29 a doorknob

30 an intercom

31 a key

INTERCOM

Word Partnerships

the ground	floor
the first	
the second	
the third	
the fourth	

Words in Action

1. Role-play with a partner. One of you is the super of this building. The other is looking for an apartment.
   - Student A: *Is there a laundry room?*
   - Student B: *Yes. It's in the basement.*

2. Describe an apartment building you know.

67

House and Garden

1

2

3

4

7

8

9

10

11

21

22

23

24

25

26

27

28

29

1 a chimney

2 an attic

3 a skylight

4 a roof

5 a deck

6 a grill / a barbecue

7 a hammock

8 a lawn / grass

9 a lawn mower

10 a window

11 a shutter

12 a door

13 a doorbell

14 a porch

15 steps

16 a garage

17 a rake

18 a driveway

19 a garbage can / a trash can

20 a yard

21 a garden

22 a patio

23 a gate

24 a fence

25 hedge clippers

26 a wheelbarrow

27 a (garden) hose

28 a walk(way)

29 a sprinkler

Word Partnerships

| a flower | garden |
| a vegetable | |

a chain-link	fence
a picket	
a barbed wire	

a front	door
a screen	
a garage	

Words in Action

1. Cover the word list. Name as many parts of the house as you can. Start at the top of the house and work your way down.

2. Draw your dream house. Label all the parts. Show your dream house to a partner. How are they similar? How are they different?

Kitchen and Dining Area

Words in Context

Before 1900, few **kitchens** had electricity. People used **candles** for light. There were no **refrigerators**, no **ovens**, no **dishwashers**, and no **blenders**. There were no faucets, either. To wash **dishes**, people had to get water from outdoors and heat it over a fire.

1	a microwave (oven)	21	a stool
2	a cabinet	22	a chair
3	dishes	23	a plate
4	a shelf	24	a bowl
5	a counter(top)	25	a glass
6	a stove	26	a placemat
7	a (tea) kettle	27	silverware
8	an oven	28	a candle
9	a potholder	29	a teapot
10	a coffeemaker	30	a mug
11	a spice rack	31	a napkin
12	a blender	32	a table
13	a toaster		
14	a dishwasher		
15	a sink		
16	a drying rack / a dish rack		
17	a garbage disposal		
18	a dish towel		
19	a freezer		
20	a refrigerator		

Word Partnerships

a dining room	table
a kitchen	chair
an electric	stove
a gas	
load	the dishwasher
start / turn on	
empty	

Words in Action

1. What do you think are the ten most important things in this kitchen? Why?
2. Work with a group. What things do all of you have in your kitchen? Make a list.

Living Room

Words in Context

Some people like lots of furniture in their living rooms—a **sofa,** a **love seat,** a **coffee table,** chairs, a **wall unit,** and several **lamps.** Others like just a rug and a couple of **easy chairs.** In the Middle East, people often sit on **cushions** or low **benches** instead of chairs. And in some Asian countries, people sit on the **floor.**

1 a bench

2 a cushion

3 an armchair /
  an easy chair

4 an end table

5 a lamp

6 a lampshade

7 a wall unit

8 a sofa / a couch

9 a (throw) pillow

10 a window seat

11 a love seat

12 a coffee table

13 an ottoman

14 the floor

15 a curtain rod

16 a (ceiling) fan

17 a ceiling

18 a smoke detector

19 blinds

20 a curtain

21 a wall

22 a bookcase

23 a vent

24 a (light) switch

25 a thermostat

26 a mantel

27 a fireplace

28 a fire screen

29 a house plant

30 a fire

31 a rocking chair

32 an outlet

Word Partnerships

a floor	lamp
a table	
a desk	
sit	in an armchair
	in a rocking chair
	on a sofa
	on the floor
	on a cushion

Words in Action

1. How is your living room similar to this one? How is it different? Discuss with a partner.
   - *I have a fireplace like the one in the picture.*
   - *My sofa is bigger than the one in the picture.*

2. Draw your perfect living room. Label all the items in the drawing.

Bedroom and Bathroom

Words in Context

Feng shui is a Chinese art. It suggests ways to make homes healthy and happy. For a calm **bedroom,** your **bed** should not face a door. Your **bedspread** should not touch the floor. In the **bathroom,** the **toilet** should not face the door. You should have many **mirrors.** Mirrors bring happiness.

1 a closet			
2 a blanket	6 a dresser	10 a night table	14 a bed
3 a carpet	7 a mirror	11 a pillowcase	15 a sheet
4 a rug	8 a (window) shade	12 a pillow	16 a comforter
5 a drawer	9 an alarm clock	13 a mattress	17 a bedspread

18	a shower	22	a (bath)tub	26	a towel	30	a toilet brush
19	a shower curtain	23	a plunger	27	a faucet	31	a wastebasket
20	a drain	24	toilet paper / toilet tissue	28	a sink		
21	a medicine cabinet	25	a toilet	29	a washcloth		

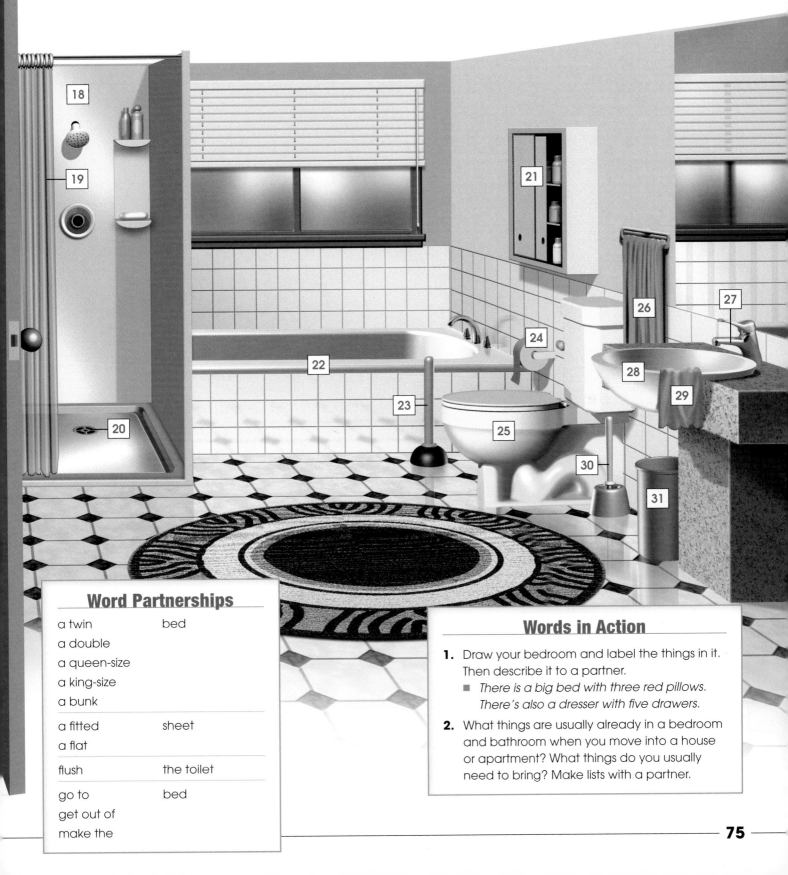

Word Partnerships

a twin	bed
a double	
a queen-size	
a king-size	
a bunk	

a fitted	sheet
a flat	

flush	the toilet

go to	bed
get out of	
make the	

Words in Action

1. Draw your bedroom and label the things in it. Then describe it to a partner.
   - *There is a big bed with three red pillows. There's also a dresser with five drawers.*

2. What things are usually already in a bedroom and bathroom when you move into a house or apartment? What things do you usually need to bring? Make lists with a partner.

Household Problems

Words in Context

A: Our kitchen sink **is clogged.**

B: Call a **plumber** right away.

A: And the power **is out.**

B: Call an **electrician.**

A: And the roof **is leaking,** too.

B: Call a real estate agent. You need a new house!

16

2 15

3

4 5 6

17

7

23 ants

24 mice

25 rats

26 termites

27 cockroaches

8

9

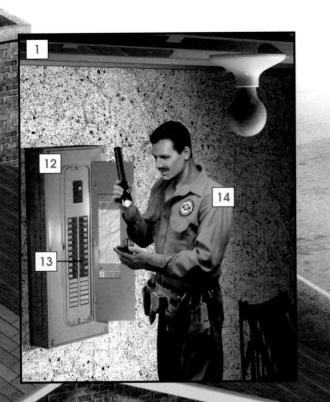

1 The power **is out.**
2 The toilet **is clogged.**
3 The roof **leaks.**
4 The wall **is cracked.**
5 The faucet **drips.**
6 The lightbulb **is burned out.**
7 The heater **doesn't work.**
8 The pipes **are frozen.**
9 The basement **is flooded.**
10 The window **is broken.**
11 The lock **is jammed.**

12 a breaker panel
13 a circuit breaker
14 an electrician
15 a plumber
16 a roofer
17 a handyman
18 an exterminator
19 a water meter
20 a gas meter
21 a meter reader
22 a locksmith

Word Partnerships

read	the meter
turn on	
shut off	
flip	the circuit breaker
replace	

Words in Action

1. Discuss these questions: What household problems did you have last year? Who did the repairs?
2. Describe a household problem. Your partner will tell you who to call.
   - Student A: *I can't open the front door. The lock is jammed.*
   - Student B: *Call a locksmith.*

PEST BE GONE

Household Chores

Words in Context

In many houses, men and women share **household chores.** For example, in some houses women **do** the cooking, and men **wash** the dishes. Sometimes women **do** the laundry, and men **fold** the clothes. Sometimes women **weed** the garden, and men **rake** the leaves. What chores do you do in your family?

1

2

3

4

5

6

7

13

14

15

16

17

18

19

BILLS TO PAY   BILLS PAID

1 make the bed

2 change the sheets

3 do the laundry

4 sweep the floor

5 fold the clothes

6 pay the bills

7 vacuum the carpet

8 dust

9 polish the furniture

10 clean the sink

11 scrub the toilet

12 mop the floor

13 empty the wastebasket

14 shake out the rug

15 weed the garden

16 wash the car

17 mow the lawn /
mow the grass

18 water the lawn

19 take out the trash /
put out the trash

20 rake the leaves

21 do the dishes /
wash the dishes

22 cook / do the cooking

23 dry the dishes

24 put away the dishes

Word Partnerships

clean	the house
	the bathroom
	your bedroom
polish	the car
	the silver
	the floor

Words in Action

1. Name two household chores you like to do and two you hate to do.

2. Work in a group. Imagine your group is a family—a mother, a father, and teenage children. Divide the household chores on the list among yourselves. Who will do what?

Cleaning Supplies

Words in Context

Do you want to wash a window? Follow these steps:

- Put on **rubber gloves.**
- Mix a gallon of warm water with a little ammonia.
- Put the liquid on the window with a clean **sponge.**
- Pull a **squeegee** across the window.
- Wipe the squeegee with a **rag** or a **paper towel** and repeat.

1 a feather duster

2 a dustpan

3 a vacuum cleaner bag

4 vacuum cleaner attachments

5 a vacuum (cleaner)

6 a squeegee

7 paper towels

8 trash bags

9 furniture polish

10 a dust cloth

11 glass cleaner

12 dishwasher detergent

13 dish soap / dishwashing liquid

14 a scouring pad

15 bug spray / insect spray

16 a bucket / a pail

17 a rag

18 rubber gloves

19 cleanser

20 a scrub brush

21 a sponge

22 a flyswatter

23 a stepladder

24 a mousetrap

25 a recycling bin

26 a mop

27 a dust mop

28 a broom

Word Partnerships

heavy-duty	trash bags
20-gallon	
plastic	
a sponge	mop
a string	
a floor	
a push	broom
a kitchen	

Words in Action

1. Name cleaning supplies you use often. What do you use each item for?

2. You need to clean your living room, your bathroom, and your kitchen. Which cleaning items will you use for each room?

Fruits and Nuts

Words in Context

Grapes are one of the most popular **fruits** in the world. Every day, millions of people enjoy them. Many people also like **apples.** Apples first came from Afghanistan. **Oranges, lemons,** and **limes** are also popular around the world. These fruits came from China.

1

2

3

4

5

11

8

9

10

19

15

16

17

18

22

23

24

25

26

27

30

31

32

33

34

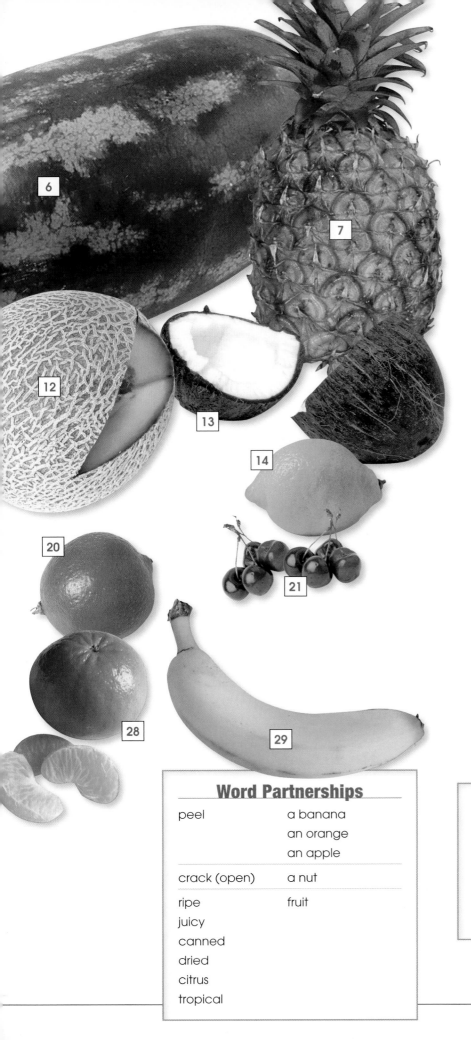

Fruits

1 a pear
2 a kiwi
3 an orange
4 a pomegranate
5 grapes
6 a watermelon
7 a pineapple
8 a mango
9 a grapefruit
10 an avocado
11 an apple
12 a cantaloupe
13 a coconut
14 a lemon
15 a plum
16 an apricot
17 blueberries
18 a papaya
19 a peach
20 a lime
21 cherries
22 figs
23 olives
24 dates
25 strawberries
26 raspberries
27 raisins
28 a tangerine
29 a banana

Nuts

30 pecans
31 almonds
32 pistachios
33 peanuts
34 walnuts

Word Partnerships

peel	a banana
	an orange
	an apple
crack (open)	a nut
ripe	fruit
juicy	
canned	
dried	
citrus	
tropical	

Words in Action

1. What are your five favorite fruits? Rank them in order. Share your list with your class. Is your list similar to other students' lists?

2. Create a recipe for a delicious fruit drink. Use at least four fruits.

Vegetables

Words in Context

Cabbage Slaw Recipe

Cut a head of **cabbage** into thin slices. Then cut a large **cucumber,** a **bell pepper,** a **carrot,** and an **onion** (or three **scallions**) into small pieces. Mix everything together with a little salt. Add a little oil and vinegar and mix everything again.

1 broccoli

2 beets

3 asparagus

4 spinach

5 lettuce

6 squash

7 a tomato

8 cabbage

9 pinto beans

10 chickpeas / garbanzo beans

11 a zucchini

12 an eggplant

13 an artichoke

14 celery

15 an onion

16 cauliflower

17 a turnip

18 kidney beans

19 a carrot

20 bean sprouts

21 lima beans

22 a sweet potato

23 a bell pepper

24 corn

25 a cucumber

26 a potato

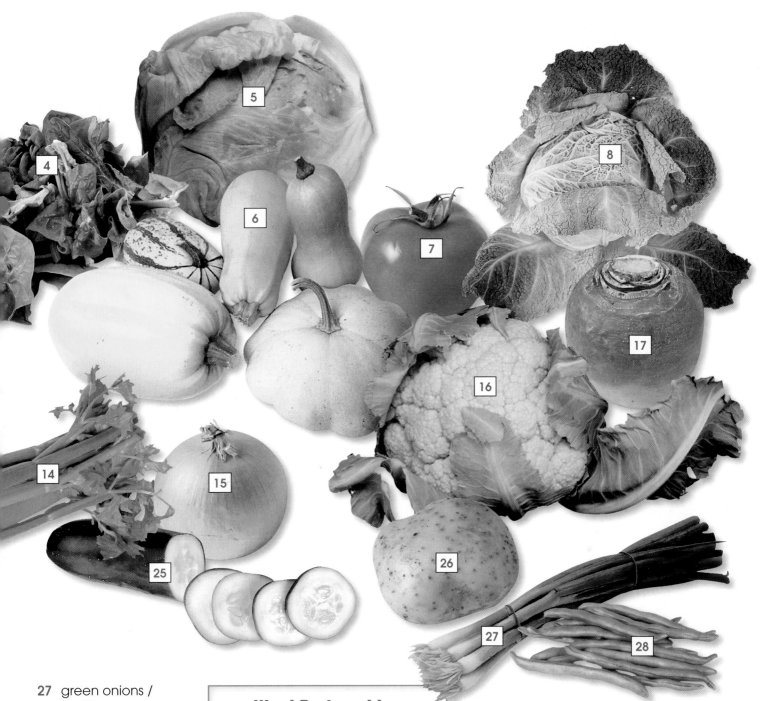

27 green onions / scallions

28 green beans / string beans

29 garlic

30 peas

31 a radish

32 a mushroom

Word Partnerships

a head of	cabbage
	cauliflower
	lettuce
an ear of	corn
a spinach	leaf
a lettuce	
fresh	vegetables
frozen	
raw	
organic	

Words in Action

1. Which vegetables do you have in your house right now? Which ones do you eat raw? Which ones have you never eaten?

2. Make two lists: *Vegetables I like* and *Vegetables I don't like*. Compare your lists with a partner.

Meat, Poultry, and Seafood

MEAT

Words in Context

Fish and **shellfish** are healthy foods. They contain very little fat. The Koreans and the Japanese eat a lot of **seafood. Clams, oysters, shrimp,** and **tuna** are favorite foods in these countries. However, Americans love **meat.** The average American eats 27 pounds (12.3 kilograms) of **ground beef** a year—mostly in hamburgers.

1

3

4

8

9

11

10

5

6

13

12

7

2

BEEF

PORK

LAMB

30

29

28

27

POULTRY

31

1 lamb chops
2 leg of lamb
3 pork chops
4 ham
5 salami
6 sausages
7 pork roast
8 ground beef
9 ribs
10 steak

11 roast beef
12 liver
13 veal cutlets
14 lobster
15 oysters
16 clams
17 mussels
18 crab
19 scallops
20 shrimp
21 filet of sole

22 cod
23 swordfish
24 salmon
25 trout
26 tuna
27 thighs
28 wings
29 breasts
30 turkey
31 chicken
32 duck
33 drumsticks / legs

Word Partnerships

raw	fish
fresh	
frozen	
grilled	
fatty	meat
lean	
a rare	steak
a medium	
a well-done	

Words in Action

1. Pick your favorite items from the meat, poultry, and seafood sections. Compare your favorites with a partner.
2. Imagine you are having a barbecue. What meat, poultry, and seafood will you buy?

Inside the Refrigerator

Words in Context

Do you want a well-organized **refrigerator**? Here are some suggestions. Keep fruit and vegetables in the drawers. Put **milk, apple juice,** and **orange juice** in the door rack. **Eggs** are safe in the egg container in the door. Always keep raw meat, poultry, and fish on the bottom shelf. **Ice cream** and **frozen vegetables** stay frozen in the freezer.

1 frozen vegetables
2 frozen waffles
3 ice cream
4 ice tray
5 soda
6 margarine
7 mayonnaise
8 sour cream
9 iced tea
10 pickles
11 tofu
12 yogurt
13 syrup
14 cream
15 bottled water
16 cake
17 jam

18 salad
19 (salad) dressing
20 bacon
21 cold cuts
22 (cheddar) cheese
23 butter
24 (Swiss) cheese
25 eggs
26 milk
27 orange juice
28 apple juice

Word Partnerships

fruit	salad
potato	
pasta	
scrambled	eggs
fried	
hard-boiled	
poached	
mozzarella	cheese
Parmesan	
cottage	

Words in Action

1. Think about the foods in the refrigerator. Make three lists: *Very healthy, Less healthy,* and *Not healthy.* Discuss your list with a partner.

2. Plan your dinner tonight using the food in this refrigerator.

Food to Go

Words in Context

Do you eat at the **food court**? Health experts have some advice for you. Don't order a **hot dog** and **french fries.** Order a salad instead. Don't have a **hamburger.** Have **beans** and **rice** instead. And finally, don't order **coffee** or soda. Have water or juice.

1 pizza	7 french fries	13 a straw
2 lasagna	8 a hot dog	14 a muffin
3 spaghetti	9 a baked potato	15 a doughnut
4 a hamburger	10 a sandwich	16 ketchup
5 a bagel	11 coffee	17 mustard
6 fish and chips	12 tea	18 chopsticks

Word Partnerships

sticky	rice
steamed	
fried	
black	beans
pinto	
refried	
a slice of	pizza
a piece of	
a small	
a medium	
a large	

19 rice

20 stir-fried vegetables

21 chicken teriyaki

22 an egg roll

23 sushi

24 soy sauce

25 a burrito

26 a taco

27 salsa

28 beans

29 a tortilla

Words in Action

1. Which take-out foods do you like? Which ones don't you like?

2. Work with a partner. Role-play ordering food at one of the places in the picture.
   - Student A: *Can I help you?*
   - Student B: *Yes, I'd like two egg rolls.*
   - Student A: *Do you want something to drink?*
   - Student B: *Yes. Coffee, please.*

Cooking

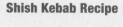

Shish Kebab Recipe

1 **Measure** $\frac{1}{4}$ cup of olive oil.

2 **Dice** 1 tablespoon of garlic.

3 **Whisk** the oil and garlic with a little lemon juice.

4 **Add** 1 pound of lamb cubes.

5 **Marinate** overnight in the refrigerator.

6 **Grill** the kebabs for 5 minutes on each side.

Breakfast Burrito Recipe

7 **Scramble** 2 eggs in a bowl.

8 **Fry** the eggs.

9 **Broil** 2 slices of bacon.

10 **Steam** a cup of broccoli.

11 **Grate** $\frac{1}{4}$ cup of cheese.

12 **Fold** everything into a tortilla.

13 **Microwave** for 30 seconds.

Roast Chicken with Potatoes Recipe

14 **Season** the chicken with garlic and rosemary.

15 **Roast** at 350°F (175°C). (20 minutes per pound)

16 **Baste** frequently with pan juices.

17 **Boil** the potatoes.

° = degrees

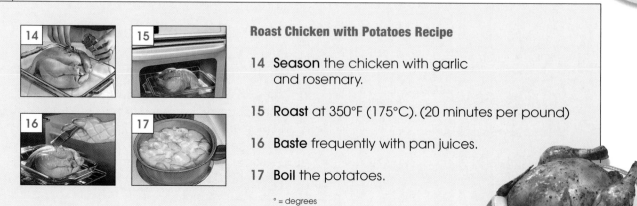

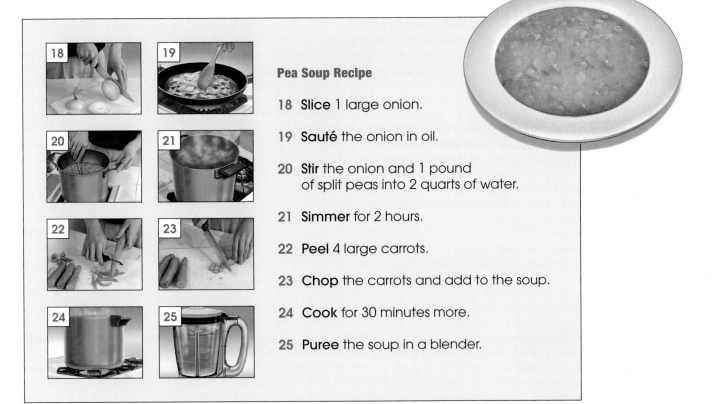

Pea Soup Recipe

18 **Slice** 1 large onion.

19 **Sauté** the onion in oil.

20 **Stir** the onion and 1 pound of split peas into 2 quarts of water.

21 **Simmer** for 2 hours.

22 **Peel** 4 large carrots.

23 **Chop** the carrots and add to the soup.

24 **Cook** for 30 minutes more.

25 **Puree** the soup in a blender.

Candy Pecans Recipe

26 **Grease** a cookie sheet.

27 **Beat** 1 egg white.

28 **Sift** $\frac{1}{2}$ cup of sugar with 2 teaspoons of cinnamon.

29 **Mix** 3 cups of pecans and the sugar and cinnamon into the egg white.

30 **Spread** the mix on a cookie sheet.

31 **Bake** at 250°F (120°C).

Word Partnerships

bake	bread
	a cake
steam	vegetables
chop	
cook	
peel	potatoes
boil	

Words in Action

1. Which recipe looks the best to you? Why?
2. Write down your favorite recipe. Put your recipe together with your classmates' recipes to make a class cookbook.

Cooking Equipment

Every country has its own **cooking equipment**. For example, Italian kitchens usually have a big **pot** for cooking pasta. Many Mexican kitchens have a special **pan** to make tortillas. Asian kitchens often have a **grill** for meat and a special **vegetable steamer**. Many kitchens around the world have a **set of knives,** a **cutting board, measuring cups,** and **measuring spoons.**

1 a cutting board	7 a (kitchen) timer	13 a grater
2 a set of knives	8 a food processor	14 a vegetable peeler
3 a (frying) pan	9 a wooden spoon	15 a bottle opener
4 a grill	10 a saucepan	16 a can opener
5 a pot	11 a ladle	17 a (meat) thermometer
6 a lid	12 a mixing bowl	18 a strainer

Word Partnerships

a cast-iron	pan
an aluminum	pot
a stainless steel	
a bread	knife
a paring	
a carving	
a sharp	
a dull	

19 a (hand) mixer

20 a whisk

21 a cookie sheet

22 a rolling pin

23 measuring cups

24 measuring spoons

25 a casserole (dish)

26 a (vegetable) steamer

27 a colander

28 a wok

29 a pie pan

30 a cake pan

31 a spatula

Words in Action

1. Which five pieces of cooking equipment do you use most often? What do you use each piece for?

2. What food do you like to cook? What cooking equipment do you need to make it?

Measurements and Containers

Words in Context

At a farmer's market, you can see a **pile** of ripe tomatoes, smell a warm **loaf** of bread, buy a **jar** of honey, and find a **bunch** of fresh carrots. You can meet the farmers who grow your food and vendors who sell **bars** of homemade soap and **bouquets** of fresh flowers.

Abbreviations

tsp.	=	teaspoon
TBS.	=	tablespoon
c.	=	cup
oz.	=	ounce
qt.	=	quart
pt.	=	pint
gal.	=	gallon
lb.	=	pound
g.	=	gram
kg.	=	kilogram
l.	=	liter

4 qt.	=	1 gal.
3 tsp.	=	1 TBS.
1 qt.	=	.94 l.
1 oz.	=	28 g.
1 lb.	=	.45 kg.

1 a pint

2 a cup

3 an ounce

4 a teaspoon

5 a tablespoon

6 a bouquet of flowers

7 a bottle of olive oil

8 a bar of soap

9 a tube of hand cream

10 a carton of orange juice

11 a tray of pastries

12 a pot of coffee

13 a cup of coffee

14 a pitcher of lemonade

15 a piece of cake

16 a loaf of bread

17 a liter of water

18 a quart of milk

19 a pound of cherries

20 a box of strawberries

21 a gallon of cider

22 a bag of potatoes

23 a carton of eggs

24 a jar of honey

25 a container of yogurt

26 a six-pack of soda

27 a can of soda

28 a pile of tomatoes

29 a bunch of carrots

30 a crate of melons

31 a basket of apples

Word Partnerships

a can of	soup
	tuna
a box of	cereal
	pasta
	cookies
a cup of	tea
	sugar
	flour
a piece of	pie
	bread

Words in Action

1. Imagine you are shopping at a farmer's market. What will you buy? Why?

2. Name five containers you have at home. Tell what is in each container.

Supermarket

1 produce

2 meats and poultry

3 dairy products

4 frozen foods

5 bakery

6 a deli counter

7 a scale

8 paper products

9 household cleaners

10 pet food

11 beverages

12 canned goods

13 an aisle

14 a paper bag

15 a checkout counter

16 a cash register

17 a shopping cart

18 a bagger

19 a barcode scanner

20 a plastic bag

21 a cashier / a checker

22 groceries

23 a shopper

24 a shopping basket

Snacks

25 a candy bar

26 pretzels

27 (potato) chips

28 popcorn

BAKERY

DELI

Word Partnerships

the frozen food	aisle
the produce	section
the canned goods	
the bakery	
shop for	groceries
pick up	

Words in Action

1. Where can you find the following items in the supermarket: *milk, water, bread, apples, paper towels, chicken,* and *ice cream*? Work with a partner.
   - *Milk is with the dairy products.*
   - *Water is in the beverages section.*

2. What section do you go to first in a supermarket? What do you get there?

Restaurant

Words in Context

The first **restaurant** opened in Paris in 1765. The only thing on the **menu** was soup. There were no **appetizers** and no **desserts.** Restaurants have changed a lot since then. Now you can eat at a Chinese restaurant in Moscow or a Mexican restaurant in Beijing. The biggest restaurant in the world is the Royal Dragon in Bangkok. The dining room seats 5,000 **diners.** The **servers** wear roller skates!

1 a chef
2 a dishwasher
3 an apron
4 a server / a waitress
5 a busser / a busboy
6 a server / a waiter
7 a diner / a customer
8 a creamer
9 a vase
10 a sugar bowl
11 a tablecloth
12 a saltshaker

13 a pepper shaker
14 a bowl
15 a wine glass
16 a (water) glass
17 a high chair
18 a cup
19 a saucer
20 a menu
21 a fork
22 a napkin
23 a plate
24 a knife

25 a spoon
26 an appetizer
27 a main course
28 a dessert
29 a tray
30 a salad bar
31 a check / a bill

Guest Check

TABLE NO.	NO. PERSONS	CHECK NO. 052173	SERVER NO.
1 coffee			$1.75
1 soda			$2.00
1 salad			$4.50
1 dinner special			$9.50
31			
		TOTAL	$17.75
THANK YOU!			

Word Partnerships

a steak	knife
a butter	
a salad	fork
a dinner	
a soup	spoon
a dessert	
a serving	
a dinner	plate
a dessert	
a soup	bowl
a salad	

Words in Action

1. Compare your favorite restaurant with this one. How is it the same? How is it different?

2. What is your favorite appetizer? Main course? Dessert?

Order, Eat, Pay

Words in Context

I'm a waitress. I **wait on** lots of customers every night. Some customers are difficult. They **order** things that aren't on the menu. They **spill** their drinks. One customer left and didn't **pay** the check! But most customers are great. Some of them **compliment** me and **leave** a big tip. They're my favorite customers!

1 make a reservation

2 pour water

3 light a candle

4 carry a tray

5 set the table

6 wait on someone

7 look at the menu

8 butter the bread

9 spill a drink

10 order

11 take an order

12 drink

13 compliment someone

14 refill the glass

15 eat

16 serve a meal

17 ask for the check

18 signal the server

19 share a dessert

20 offer a doggie bag

21 thank the server

22 wipe the table

23 leave a tip

24 pay the check

25 clear the table / bus the table

Clothes

Words in Context

The **clothes** we wear today come from around the world. For example, the **tie** is originally from Croatia. The **poncho** is from South America. The **business suit** originated in France in the 1700s. And a Bavarian immigrant named Levi Strauss made the first **blue jeans** in California in 1873. Now blue jeans are popular around the world.

1 a dress

2 a shirt

3 a sweatshirt

4 sweatpants

5 a gown

6 a tuxedo

7 a windbreaker

8 shorts

9 a sari

10 a raincoat

11 a poncho

12 overalls

13 a uniform

14 a blouse

15 a skirt

16 a jacket

17 a hat

18 a scarf

19 a trench coat

20 a pullover / a sweater

21 a sports jacket / a sports coat

22 pants / trousers / slacks

23 a shawl

24 a maternity dress

25 a T-shirt

26 a vest

27 (blue) jeans

28 a tie

29 a (business) suit

30 a coat

Word Partnerships

a leather	jacket
a down	coat
a winter	
a cowboy	hat
a sun	
a straw	
a silk	blouse
	tie

Words in Action

1. Work with a partner. One person says a kind of clothing. The other person points to the clothing in the picture. Take turns.

2. Choose three or four people in your class. Say what each person is wearing.

Sleepwear, Underwear, and Swimwear

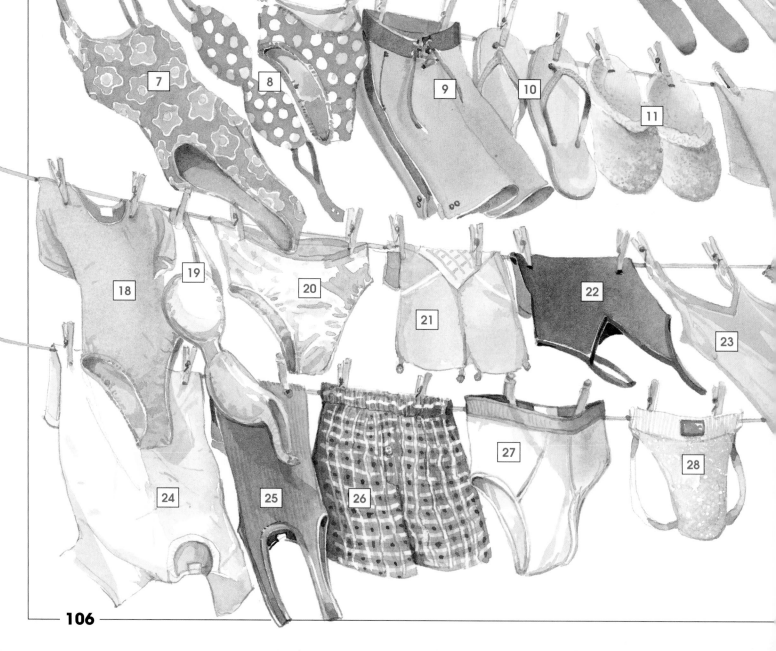

1 a clothesline

2 a clothespin

3 socks

4 tights

5 pantyhose / nylons

6 stockings

7 a swimsuit /
 a bathing suit

8 a bikini

9 (swimming) trunks

10 flip flops / thongs

11 slippers

12 a nightshirt

13 a (bath)robe

14 a nightgown

15 long underwear

16 a (blanket) sleeper

17 pajamas

18 a leotard

19 a bra

20 panties / underpants

21 a girdle

22 a camisole

23 a slip

24 an undershirt

25 a tank top

26 boxer shorts / boxers

27 briefs

28 an athletic supporter /
 a jockstrap

Word Partnerships

a terrycloth	(bath)robe
a silk	
a flannel	
knee	socks
sweat	
ankle	
dress	
a pair of	briefs
	boxer shorts
	socks
	slippers

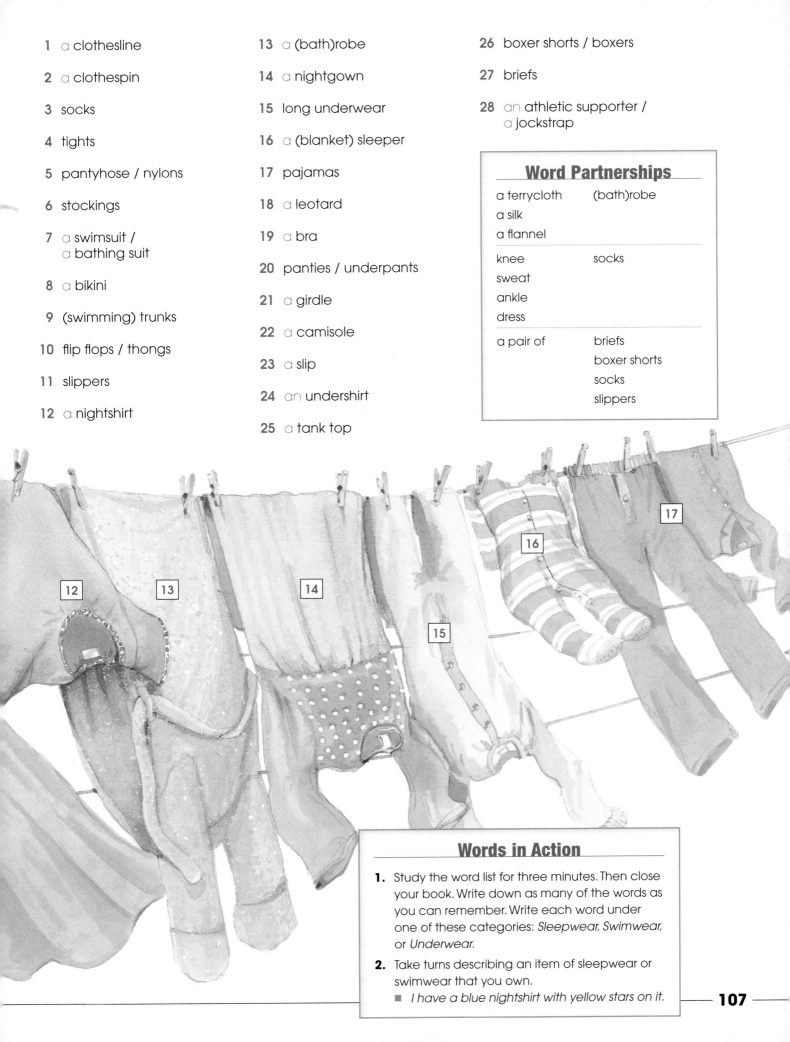

Words in Action

1. Study the word list for three minutes. Then close your book. Write down as many of the words as you can remember. Write each word under one of these categories: *Sleepwear*, *Swimwear*, or *Underwear*.

2. Take turns describing an item of sleepwear or swimwear that you own.

 ■ *I have a blue nightshirt with yellow stars on it.*

107

Shoes and Accessories

Word Partnerships

a pair of	shoes
comfortable	shoes
walking	
running	
tennis	
a gold	ring
an engagement	
a wedding	
a diamond	
pierced	earrings
clip-on	
pearl	

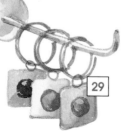

1 gloves

2 a purse / a handbag

3 mittens

4 an umbrella

5 suspenders

6 a belt

7 a ring

8 a necklace

9 earrings

10 a bracelet

11 a (wrist)watch

12 a pin

13 jewelry

14 sunglasses

15 a wallet

16 a briefcase

17 a (high) heel

18 a pump

19 a loafer

20 a clog

21 a sandal

22 a sneaker

23 an athletic shoe

24 a hiking boot

25 a boot

26 a (knit) hat

27 a baseball cap / a baseball hat

28 earmuffs

29 a key chain

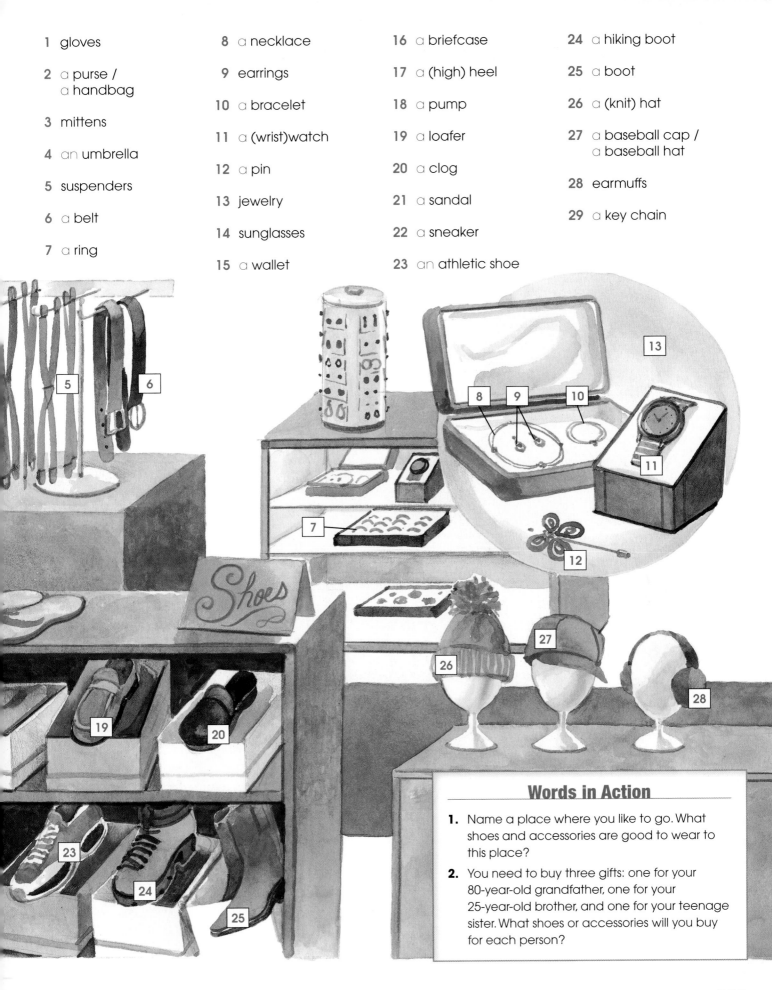

Words in Action

1. Name a place where you like to go. What shoes and accessories are good to wear to this place?

2. You need to buy three gifts: one for your 80-year-old grandfather, one for your 25-year-old brother, and one for your teenage sister. What shoes or accessories will you buy for each person?

Describing Clothes

1
2
3
4
5
8
9
10
11
12

Word Partnerships

fashionable	clothes
trendy	
designer	
work	
maternity	

7:00
Casual Clothes
24

8:00
Formal Clothes
25

1 a light jacket

2 a heavy jacket

3 a sleeveless shirt

4 a short-sleeved shirt

5 a long-sleeved shirt

6 a button-down shirt

7 a polo shirt

8 a wide tie

9 a narrow tie

10 flared jeans

11 straight leg jeans

12 baggy pants / loose pants

13 a V-neck sweater

14 a crew neck sweater

15 a cardigan sweater

16 a turtleneck sweater

17 a tight skirt

18 a straight skirt

19 a pleated skirt

20 a short skirt

21 a long skirt

22 high heels

23 low heels

24 informal clothes / casual clothes

25 formal clothes / dress clothes

Words in Action

1. Describe the clothes you and other people in class are wearing.

2. Which items of clothing in the picture are in fashion? Are any of the clothes not in fashion?

Fabrics and Patterns

Words in Context

Fabrics can be natural or man-made. **Linen, cotton,** and **silk** are natural fabrics. Linen and cotton come from plants. Silk comes from silk worms. Polyester is a man-made fabric. It is made from chemicals. It is now the most common fabric in the world.

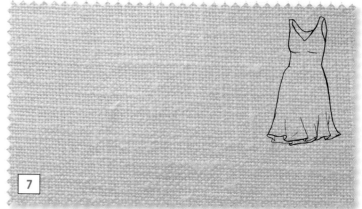

1

2

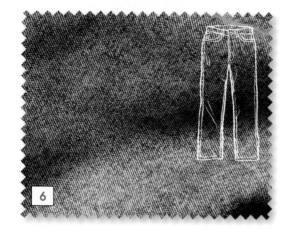

3

4

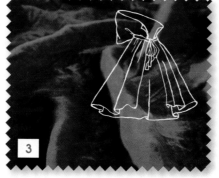

7

6

10

Word Partnerships

a wool	jacket
	sweater
	coat
	scarf
a silk	tie
	robe
	dress

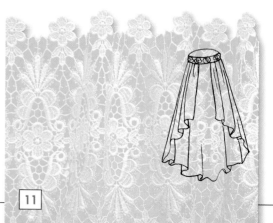

11

Fabrics

1 cotton
2 corduroy
3 velvet
4 silk
5 leather
6 denim
7 linen
8 suede
9 cashmere
10 nylon
11 lace
12 wool

Patterns

13 solid
14 print
15 polka dot
16 floral
17 paisley
18 checked
19 plaid
20 striped
21 embroidered

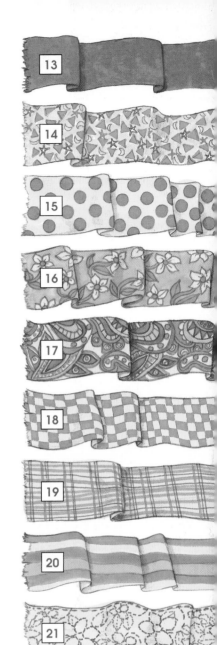

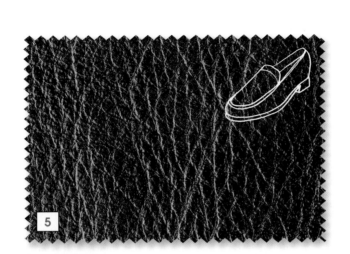

Words in Action

1. Work with a partner. Describe your partner's clothes.
   ■ *You're wearing brown corduroy pants and a blue and white striped cotton shirt.*

2. Design an outfit. Decide on the fabrics and patterns. Draw the outfit and describe it to your class.

Buying, Wearing, and Caring for Clothes

Words in Context

Different clothes have different care instructions. Jeans are easy. You can **wash** them in the washing machine and then **dry** them in the dryer. However, a wool shirt needs special care. You shouldn't wash a wool shirt. Instead, you should **dry clean** it. To prevent wrinkles, always **hang up** clothes.

1 go shopping	5 buy	10 button	15 unzip
2 look for a jacket	6 take home	11 buckle	16 unbuckle
3 go into a dressing room	7 cut off	12 roll up	17 take off
4 try on	8 put on	13 wear	18 wash
	9 zip	14 unbutton	19 dry

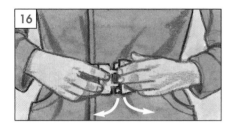

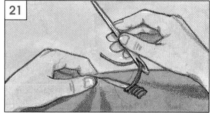

20 dry clean

21 mend / repair

22 sew on

23 iron / press

24 hang (up)

Word Partnerships

hang it	on a hook
	on a hanger
	in the closet
wash it	in cold water
	in hot water
	by hand
zip	up
button	

Words in Action

1. Pretend to do one of the actions on the word list. Your partner will guess what you are doing. Take turns.

2. Explain how you care for your favorite piece of clothing.
   - *I never wash my leather jacket in the washing machine. I dry clean it.*

Sewing and Laundry

Words in Context

Fashion designer Josie Natori comes from the Philippines. She sells her clothes all over the world. Her company started very small. At first, Natori worked alone in her living room with a **sewing machine, pins, needles, buttons, thread,** and **scissors.** Now her company has offices in Manila, Paris, and New York.

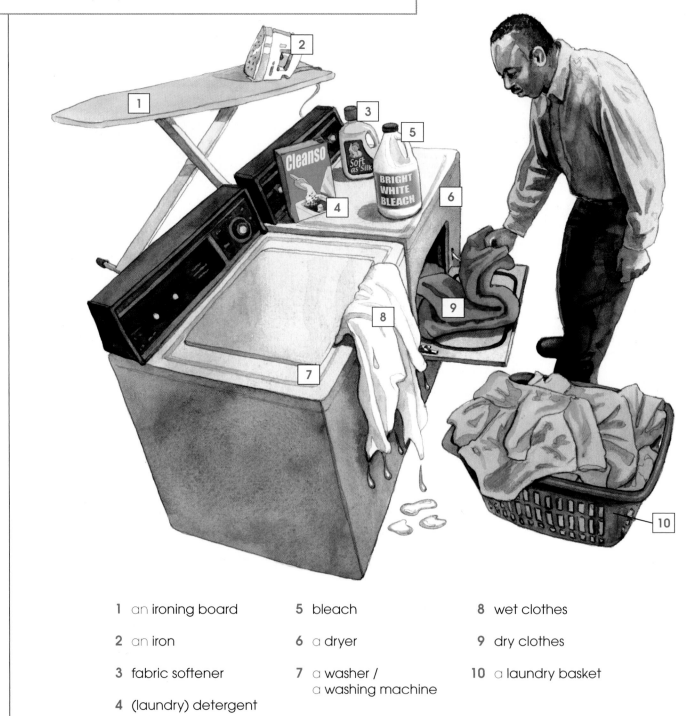

1 an ironing board

2 an iron

3 fabric softener

4 (laundry) detergent

5 bleach

6 a dryer

7 a washer /
   a washing machine

8 wet clothes

9 dry clothes

10 a laundry basket

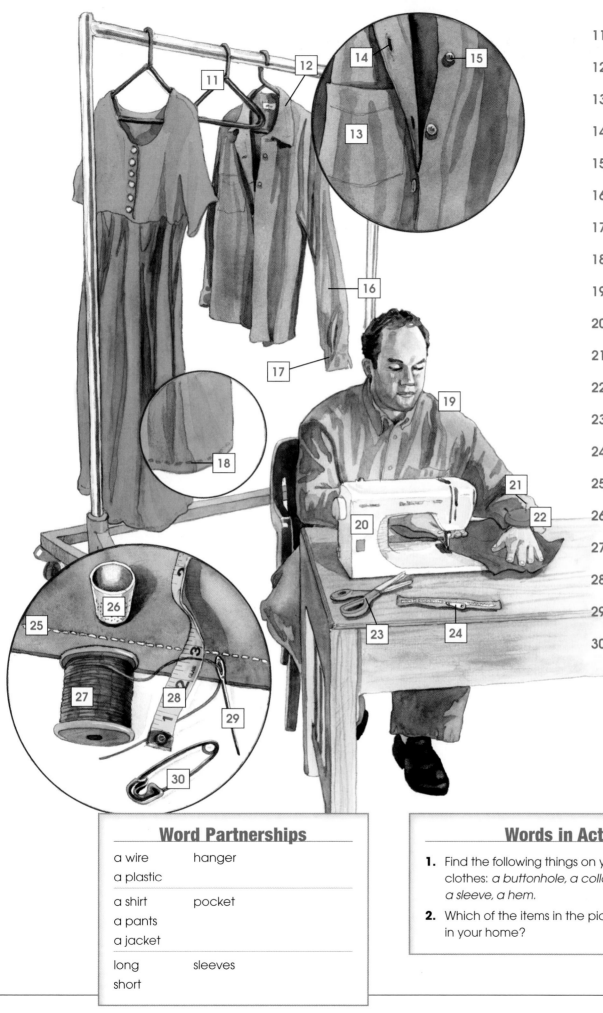

11 a hanger

12 a collar

13 a pocket

14 a buttonhole

15 a button

16 a sleeve

17 a cuff

18 a hem

19 a tailor

20 a sewing machine

21 a pin

22 a pincushion

23 a (pair of) scissors

24 a zipper

25 a seam

26 a thimble

27 thread

28 a tape measure

29 a needle

30 a safety pin

Word Partnerships

a wire	hanger
a plastic	
a shirt	pocket
a pants	
a jacket	
long	sleeves
short	

Words in Action

1. Find the following things on your classmates' clothes: *a buttonhole, a collar, a cuff, a pocket, a sleeve, a hem.*

2. Which of the items in the picture do you have in your home?

Vehicles and Traffic Signs

Words in Context

Do you need a new car or truck? There is a lot to think about. Do you have children? A **compact car** may be too small. People with children often drive large **vehicles** like **station wagons, sedans,** and **SUVs.** Do you like to camp? An **RV** may be good for you. Do you like adventure? You might like a **motorcycle.** Do you often need to move large things? You may want a **pickup truck.** There are so many vehicles to choose from!

1

 2

 3

 4

5

 6

 7

8

 9

10

11

Signs

1 one way

2 stop

3 hospital

4 do not pass

5 do not enter

6 no left turn

7 railroad crossing

8 school zone

9 pedestrian crossing

10 yield

11 no U-turn

Vehicles

12 a school bus

13 a tow truck

14 a garbage truck

15 a pickup (truck)

16 an RV

17 a minivan

18 a limousine / a limo

19 a sedan

20 a van

21 a dump truck

22 an SUV

23 a trailer

24 a sports car

25 a semi /
   a tractor trailer

26 a police car

27 an ambulance

28 a fire engine

29 a station wagon

30 a compact (car)

31 a convertible

32 a motorcycle

Word Partnerships

drive	a convertible
	a truck
	an SUV
ride	a motorcycle
ride in	a limousine
ride on	a bus

Words in Action

1. Work with a partner. Make a list of the five largest vehicles in the word list. Make another list of the five smallest vehicles.

2. Imagine you have enough money to buy a new vehicle. What vehicle will you buy? Explain your choice to the class.

Parts of a Car

1

2

3

4

5

6

7

GOGRT22
NORTH DAKOTA

8

9

10

11

12

13

14

15

E   F

16

17

18

19

20

21

22

23

24

25

26

27

28

120

1 a child car seat

2 a jack

3 a trunk

4 a tire

5 a taillight

6 a brake light

7 a gas tank

8 a license plate

9 a bumper

10 an air bag

11 a rearview mirror

12 a seat belt

13 an oil gauge

14 a speedometer

15 a gas gauge

16 a dashboard

17 a radio

18 a glove compartment

19 air conditioning

20 heater

21 a horn

22 an ignition

23 a gearshift

24 a steering wheel

25 a clutch

26 a brake pedal

27 an accelerator / a gas pedal

28 an emergency brake

29 a windshield wiper

30 a hood

31 a fender

32 an engine / a motor

33 a battery

34 jumper cables

35 a radiator

36 a turn signal

37 a headlight

Word Partnerships

open	the hood
close	the trunk
check	the battery
	the rearview mirror
a spare	tire
a flat	

Words in Action

1. Study the word list for three minutes. Then close your book. Write down as many of the words as you can remember. Write each word under one of these categories: *Inside the car,* *Outside the car,* and *Under the hood.* Compare your lists with a partner.

2. Draw a car. Label as many parts of the car as you can, without looking at the word list.

Road Trip

Words in Context

Here are some tips for a good **road trip.** Before you **leave,** make sure your car is running well. **Get** gas, **check** the oil, and **put** air in your tires. Take plenty of coins to **pay** tolls. Once you are on the road, **turn on** your headlights. Finally, make sure you **get off** the highway for a short break every two or three hours.

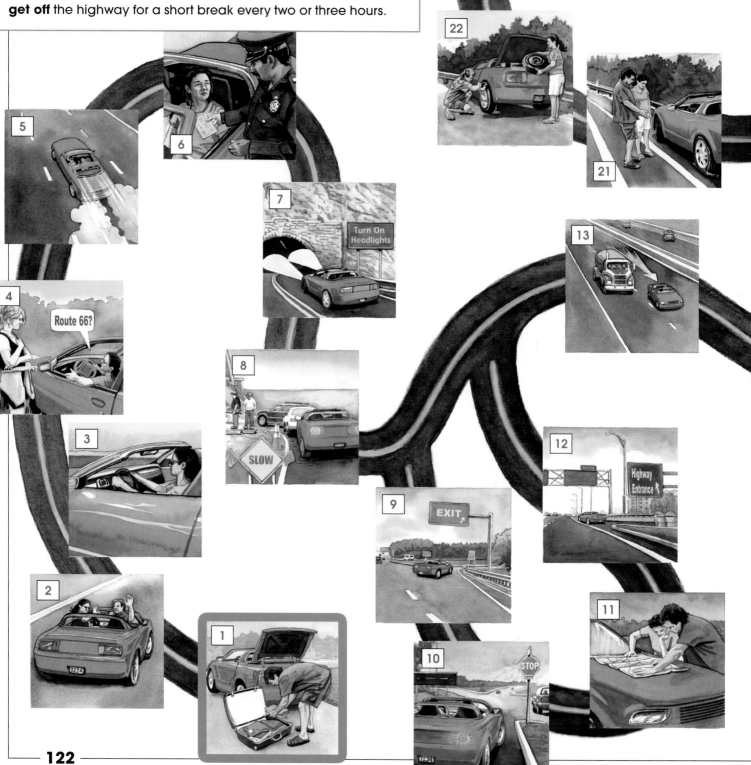

1 pack
2 leave
3 drive
4 ask for directions
5 speed up
6 get a speeding ticket
7 turn on the headlights
8 slow down

9 get off the highway
10 stop
11 look at a map
12 get on the highway
13 pass a truck
14 honk (the horn)
15 get gas
16 check the oil
17 wash the windshield
18 put air in the tires
19 have an accident
20 pull over
21 have a flat (tire)
22 change the tire
23 pay a toll
24 arrive at the destination
25 park (the car)

Word Partnerships

pack	a suitcase
	a bag
stop	at a red light
	for gas
turn on	the windshield wipers
	the radio
	the air conditioning

Words in Action

1. Work with a partner. Act out a verb on the list. Your partner will guess the verb. Take turns.

2. Plan your "dream" road trip. Where will you go? What will you do on the trip?

Airport

Words in Context

Air travel is changing. **Airports** now have **automated check-in machines.** A **passenger** can quickly check in, choose a **seat,** and get a **boarding pass.** In the future, some **airplanes** will be bigger and some will fly much faster.

9 a metal detector

10 a security checkpoint

11 arrival and departure monitors

12 a helicopter

13 a runway

14 a gate

15 a pilot

16 a carry-on bag

17 customs

18 a customs (declaration) form

19 the baggage claim (area)

20 immigration

21 a line

Airplane / Plane

22 first class

23 economy (class) / coach (class)

24 an overhead compartment

25 an emergency exit

26 a flight attendant

27 a seat

28 a seat belt

29 an aisle

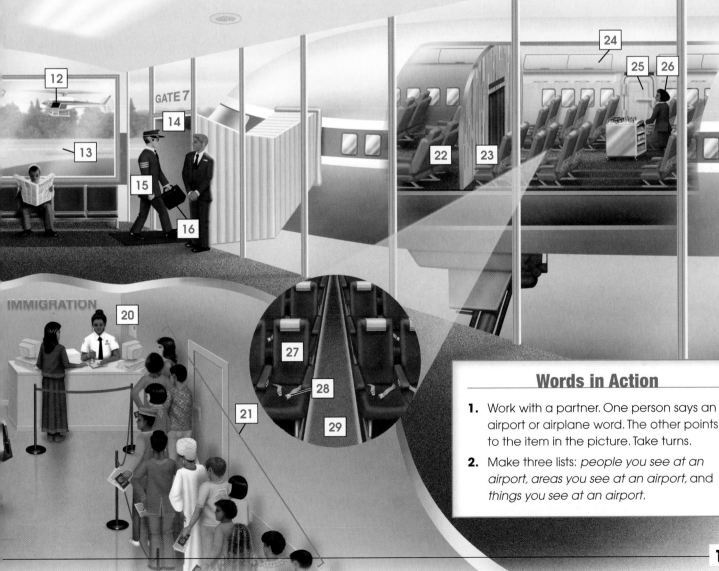

Words in Action

1. Work with a partner. One person says an airport or airplane word. The other points to the item in the picture. Take turns.

2. Make three lists: *people you see at an airport, areas you see at an airport,* and *things you see at an airport.*

Taking a Flight

Words in Context

Air Travel Tips

- **Check in** early.
- When you **board** the plane, **stow** your carry-on bag.
- Drink plenty of water.
- **Stretch** often.
- **Ask for** a pillow. Put your seat back, and try to sleep as much as possible.

1 check in

2 show your ID

3 check your baggage

4 get your boarding pass

5 go through security

6 check the monitors

7 wait at the gate

8 board the plane

9 find your seat

10 stow your carry-on bag

11 turn off your cell phone

12 fasten your seat belt

13 take off

14 ask for a pillow

15 turn on the overhead light

16 put on your headphones

17 listen to music

18 put your tray table down

19 stretch

20 choose a meal

21 land

22 unfasten your seat belt

23 get off the plane

24 claim your bags

126

Pillow, please.

Word Partnerships

wait	for a boarding call
	in line
go through	a metal detector
	customs
	immigration

Words in Action

1. Work with a partner. Pretend to do one of the actions on the word list. Your partner will guess what action you are doing. Take turns.

2. Make a list of things you can do on a plane to be safe. Make another list of things you can do to be comfortable.

Public Transportation

Words in Context

There are three ways to get from JFK Airport in New York to Manhattan. The first way is by **cab.** You can get a cab at the **taxi stand.** The **fare** is about $35.00. The second way is by **bus.** You can catch a bus from the **bus stop** outside the airport. The **ticket** is about $13.00. The bus will take you to a Manhattan **train station** or hotel. The third way is by **subway.** Go to the JFK Airport **subway station.** The subway will take you into Manhattan. This is the cheapest way. It costs only $2.00.

1   a taxi stand

2   a meter

3   the fare

4   a taxi / a cab

5   a taxi driver / a cab driver

6   a passenger

7   a bus stop

8   a bus driver

9   a bus

10   a ticket window

11   a ticket

12   a train

13   a conductor

14   a track

15   a strap

16   a (subway) line

17   a ferry

18   a subway (train)

19   a platform

20   a token

21   a fare card

22   a schedule

23   a turnstile

TO TRAIN AND SUBWAY

BUS STOP

7

New York City Bus 827

8

9

12

13

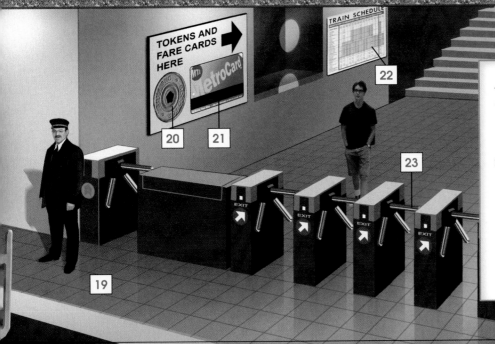

TOKENS AND FARE CARDS HERE

MTA MetroCard

TRAIN SCHEDULE

22

20 **21**

23

19

Words in Action

1. What kind of public transportation do you use? Where do you get on? What is the fare?

2. One student names a form of public transportation. Other students make up sentences about that form of transportation in your town or city.
   - Student A: *the subway*
   - Student B: *You need a fare card.*
   - Student C: *There's a subway station a block from the school.*

Up, Over, Around

Words in Context

Roller coaster rides are exciting. You go **up** a track very, very slowly. Then suddenly you go **over** the top and race **down** the track. Most roller coaster rides go **around** several sharp curves. Some even go **upside down.** But when the ride is over, people often want to do it again!

1 straight

2 past the house

3 into the tunnel

4 through the tunnel

5 out of the tunnel

6 behind the building

7 toward the rocks

8 between the flags

9 around the trees

10 up

11 down

12 upside down

13 under the waterfall

14 over the water

15 left

16 right

17 across the river

18 along the river

19 north

20 east

21 south

22 west

Word Partnerships

go	through
	straight
	across
turn	left
make a	right
take a	

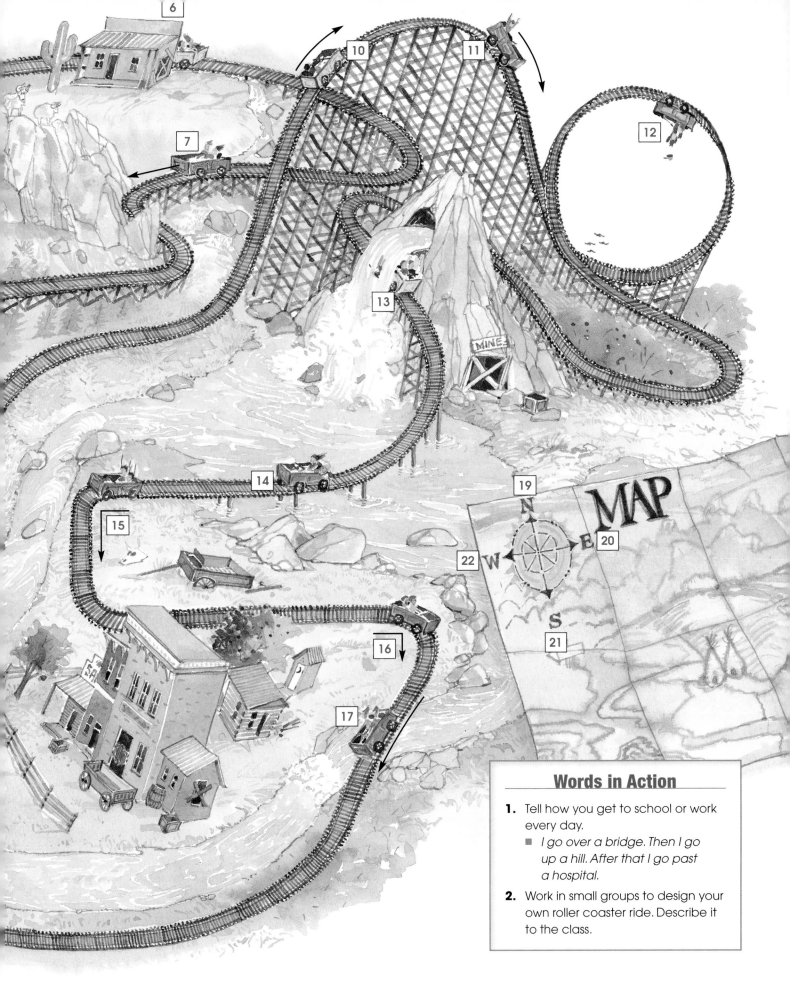

Words in Action

1. Tell how you get to school or work every day.
   - *I go over a bridge. Then I go up a hill. After that I go past a hospital.*

2. Work in small groups to design your own roller coaster ride. Describe it to the class.

The Human Body

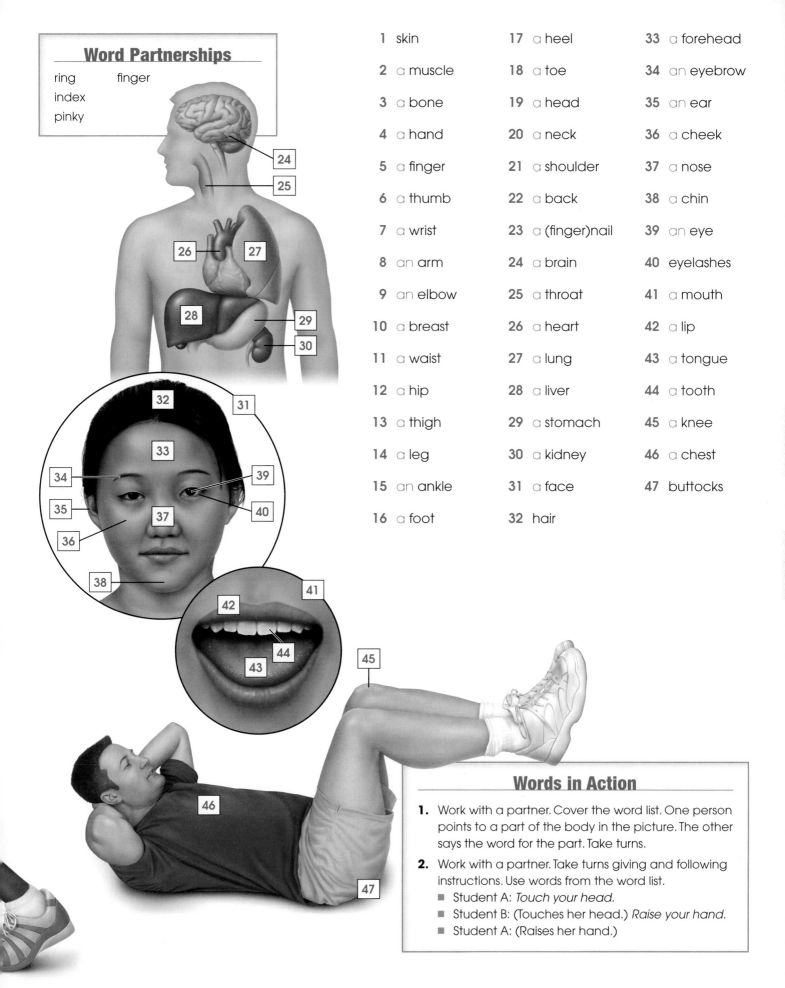

1 skin

2 a muscle

3 a bone

4 a hand

5 a finger

6 a thumb

7 a wrist

8 an arm

9 an elbow

10 a breast

11 a waist

12 a hip

13 a thigh

14 a leg

15 an ankle

16 a foot

17 a heel

18 a toe

19 a head

20 a neck

21 a shoulder

22 a back

23 a (finger)nail

24 a brain

25 a throat

26 a heart

27 a lung

28 a liver

29 a stomach

30 a kidney

31 a face

32 hair

33 a forehead

34 an eyebrow

35 an ear

36 a cheek

37 a nose

38 a chin

39 an eye

40 eyelashes

41 a mouth

42 a lip

43 a tongue

44 a tooth

45 a knee

46 a chest

47 buttocks

Words in Action

1. Work with a partner. Cover the word list. One person points to a part of the body in the picture. The other says the word for the part. Take turns.

2. Work with a partner. Take turns giving and following instructions. Use words from the word list.
   - Student A: *Touch your head.*
   - Student B: (Touches her head.) *Raise your hand.*
   - Student A: (Raises her hand.)

133

Illnesses, Injuries, Symptoms, and Disabilities

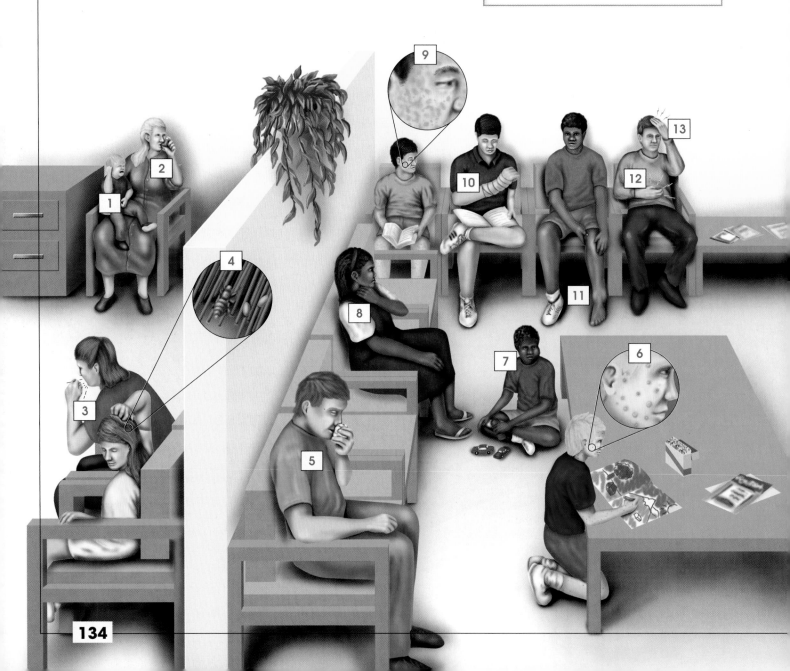

1 an earache

2 asthma

3 a cough

4 lice

5 a cold

6 chicken pox

7 mumps

8 a sore throat

9 measles

10 a sprained wrist

11 a swollen ankle

12 a stomachache

13 a headache

14 the flu

15 a fever / a temperature

16 arthritis

17 a backache

18 blind

19 nauseous

20 dizzy

21 deaf

22 acne

23 a cut

24 a burn

25 a blister

26 a rash

27 a sunburn

28 a bee sting

29 a bloody nose

30 a bruise

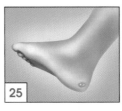

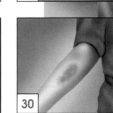

Words in Action

1. Which of the illnesses on the list can you catch from another person?

2. Make a list of three items on the list that are injuries and three that are illnesses.

Dr. Cho
Dr. Weiss
Dr. Aziz

Hurting and Healing

1	be in pain	7	choke	13	have a heart attack
2	be unconscious	8	cut yourself	14	get a(n electric) shock
3	bleed	9	drown	15	fall
4	be in shock	10	swallow poison		
5	break a leg	11	overdose (on drugs)		
6	burn yourself	12	have an allergic reaction		

Word Partnerships

be	injured	
	hurt	
feel	much	better
	a little	

16 cough	23 check his blood pressure
17 sneeze	24 draw his blood
18 vomit / throw up	25 give him a shot
19 take your temperature	26 rest
20 call the doctor	27 take a pill
21 make an appointment	28 drink fluids
22 examine the patient	29 feel better

Words in Action

1. Look at page 136. Which things on the list are more likely to happen to adults? Which are more likely to happen to children?

2. Work with a partner. One person pretends to have one of the medical problems on the list. The other guesses the problem. Take turns.

Hospital

1 a nurses' station
2 a nurse
3 an intensive care unit
4 an IV / an intravenous drip
5 an operating room
6 an X-ray
7 an anesthesiologist
8 an operating table
9 blood

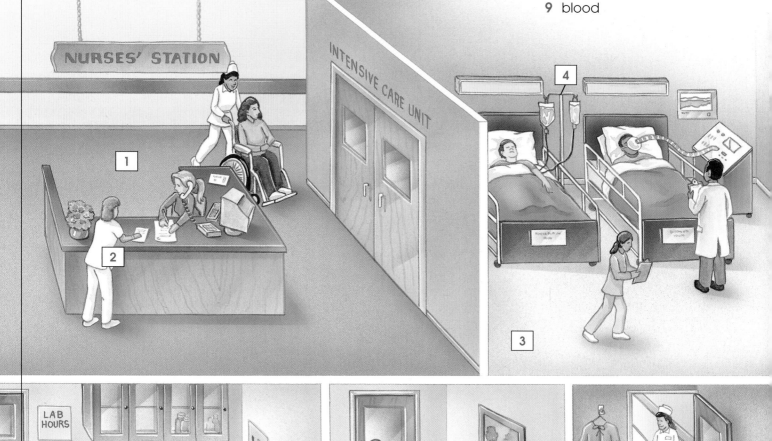

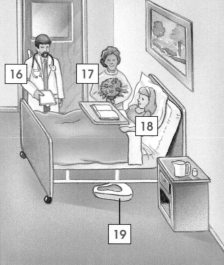

10 a surgeon

11 an operation

12 latex gloves

13 a (surgical) mask

14 a lab / a laboratory

15 a lab technician

16 a doctor

17 a visitor

18 a patient

19 a bedpan

20 a hospital gown

21 a call button

22 an orderly

23 a wheelchair

24 CPR / cardiopulmonary resuscitation

25 an emergency room

26 a paramedic / an EMT

27 a stretcher

28 stitches

29 an ambulance

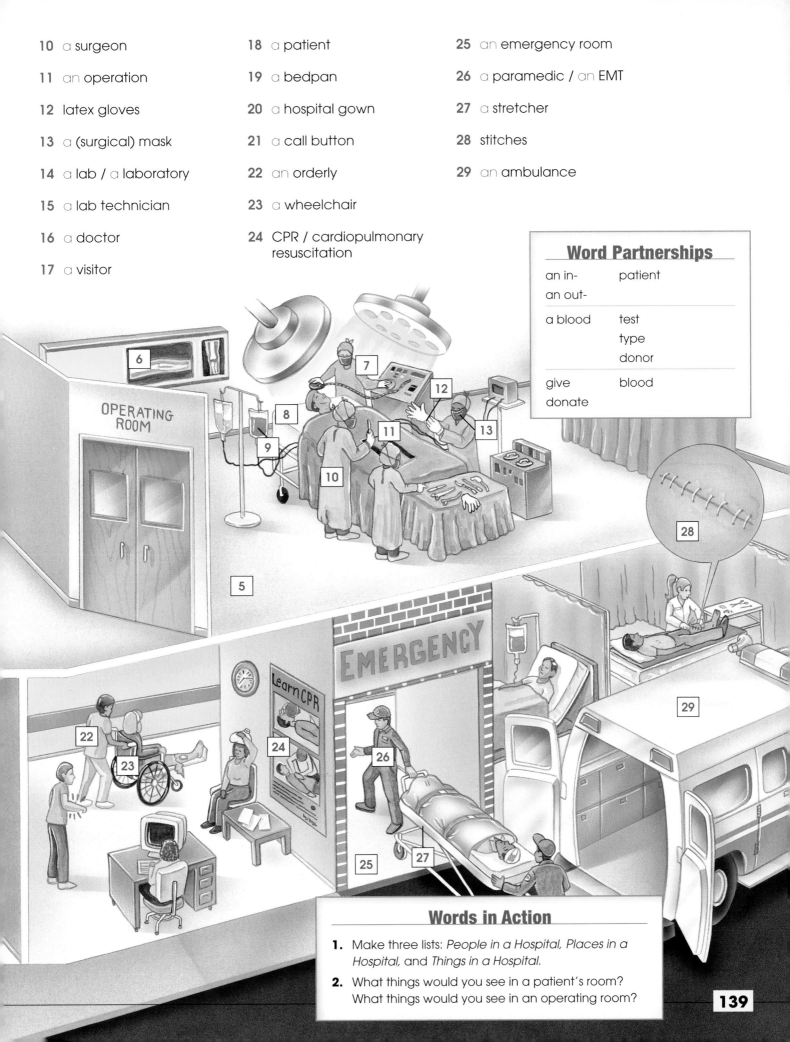

Word Partnerships

an in-	patient
an out-	
a blood	test
	type
	donor
give	blood
donate	

Words in Action

1. Make three lists: *People in a Hospital, Places in a Hospital,* and *Things in a Hospital.*

2. What things would you see in a patient's room? What things would you see in an operating room?

139

Medical Center

1

2

Words in Context

During a **physical**, a doctor does several tests. She listens to the patient's heart and lungs with a **stethoscope.** She checks the patient's blood pressure with a **blood pressure monitor.** For patients over 40, the doctor may also give the patient an **EKG.**

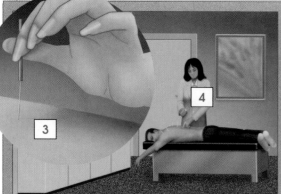

4

3

5

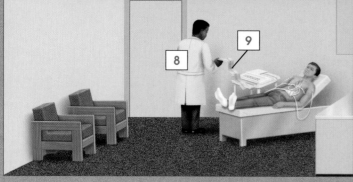

8

9

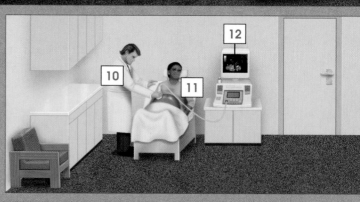

12

10

11

20

18

19

22

23

24

21

Word Partnerships

hard	contacts / contact lenses
soft	
disposable	
a leg	cast
an arm	
an annual	physical
a dental	checkup

1 a stethoscope
2 a medical chart
3 acupuncture
4 an acupuncturist
5 a psychologist
6 a waiting room
7 a pediatrician
8 a cardiologist

9 an EKG /
an electrocardiogram
10 an obstetrician
11 a pregnant woman
12 a sonogram /
an ultrasound
13 a sling
14 a crutch
15 a cast

16 a receptionist
17 an orthopedist
18 a physical (exam) /
a checkup
19 a blood pressure
monitor
20 a GP /
a general practitioner
21 an eye chart
22 a contact (lens)
23 an optometrist
24 (eye)glasses
25 a (dental) hygienist
26 a dentist
27 a filling
28 a tooth
29 braces
30 gums
31 a drill
32 a cavity

Words in Action

1. Work with a partner. Cover the word list. One person points to a person or object in the picture. The other says the word for the person or object. Take turns.

2. Work with a group. Make three lists. Who in your group has had a cast? Who has had a sling? Who has had crutches?

Pharmacy

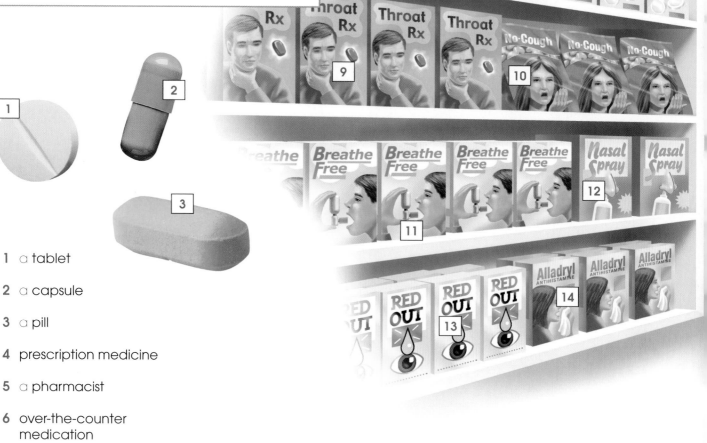

1 a tablet

2 a capsule

3 a pill

4 prescription medicine

5 a pharmacist

6 over-the-counter medication

7 cough syrup

8 an antacid

9 (throat) lozenges

10 cough drops

11 an inhaler

12 a nasal (decongestant) spray

13 eyedrops

14 antihistamine

15 a prescription

16 a warning label

17 a cane

18 a knee brace

19 an elastic bandage

20 vitamins

21 a heating pad

22 hydrogen peroxide

take	medicine
	a vitamin
	a pill
use	eyedrops
	a thermometer
	a heating pad
fill	a prescription

Do not drink

23 a first-aid kit

24 gauze

25 a sterile pad

26 sterile tape

27 aspirin

28 an adhesive bandage

29 antibacterial ointment / antibacterial cream

30 a thermometer

31 tweezers

32 a humidifier

33 an ice pack

Words in Action

1. Which pharmacy items on the word list do you have in your home?

2. Which pharmacy items are good for a cold? Which are good for a cut? Which are good for a sprain? Discuss with a partner.

143

Soap, Comb, and Floss

1 hairspray

2 shampoo

3 conditioner

4 hair gel

5 a curling iron

6 a blow dryer / a hair dryer

7 a barrette

8 a comb

9 rollers / curlers

10 a (hair)brush

11 nail polish

12 a nail clipper

13 dental floss

14 toothpaste

15 a toothbrush

16 shaving cream

17 aftershave

18 a razor

19 an electric shaver / an electric razor

20 deodorant

21 perfume

22 sunscreen

23 lotion

24 soap

25 tissues

Makeup

26 face powder

27 lipstick

28 blush / rouge

29 eye shadow

30 mascara

31 eyeliner

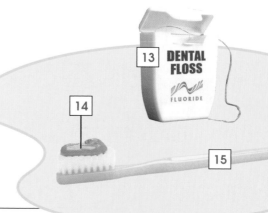

Verbs

32 wash

33 rinse

34 comb

35 (blow) dry

36 brush

37 cut

Word Partnerships

a disposable	razor
a dull	
nail polish	remover
hand	soap
face	
antibacterial	
hand	lotion
body	
put on	aftershave
wear	mascara
	lipstick

Words in Action

1. What things from the list do you use every day?
2. Work with a partner. One person pretends to use one of the items from the list. The other guesses what it is. Take turns.

Jobs 1

Words in Context

What kind of work is right for you? Do you like to work with your hands? You could be a **carpenter,** an **assembler,** or a **construction worker.** Do you want to help people? You could be a **babysitter,** a **home health aide,** or a **doctor.** Are you creative? You could be a **hairstylist,** a **florist,** or an **architect.** Are you good with numbers? You could be an **accountant** or an **engineer.**

1 an accountant	9 a delivery person	17 a barber
2 a dentist	10 a computer technician	18 an assembler
3 an artist	11 a janitor / a custodian	19 an architect
4 a cook	12 a doctor	20 a butcher
5 a hairstylist / a hairdresser	13 a homemaker	21 a (home) health aide / a (home) attendant
6 a construction worker	14 a florist	22 an engineer
7 a graphic artist	15 a housekeeper	23 a businessman / a businesswoman
8 a gardener	16 an editor	

Word Partnerships

a	part-time	job
	well-paid	
	blue-collar	
	white-collar	
look for	a job	
apply for		
get		
lose		

24 a cashier

25 an actor

26 a carpenter

27 an electrician

28 a firefighter

29 a garment worker

30 a babysitter

Words in Action

1. Look at the list. What are the best five jobs to have? Why?

2. Which jobs are done in offices? Which are done in shops? Which are done outdoors? Make three lists.

147

Jobs 2

Words in Context

There are many **jobs** in my family. I'm a **reporter** for a newspaper. My sister is a **musician.** My brother likes to work with animals, so he is a **veterinarian.** My other brother travels a lot. He's a **truck driver.** Our parents are **teachers.** They taught us to love work.

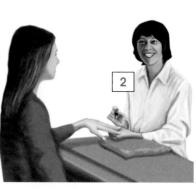

1 a reporter
2 a manicurist
3 a lawyer
4 a soldier
5 a receptionist
6 a physical therapist
7 a locksmith
8 a security guard
9 a teacher / an instructor

10 a mechanic
11 a police officer
12 a photographer
13 a stockbroker
14 a (house)painter
15 a plumber
16 a scientist
17 a taxi driver
18 a server
19 a nurse

20 a realtor
21 a salesperson
22 a tour guide
23 a pilot
24 a musician
25 a writer
26 a truck driver
27 a travel agent
28 a veterinarian / vet

Word Partnerships

a fashion	photographer
a wedding	
a registered	nurse
a school	
a commercial	pilot
a private	
a fighter	

SECURITY

HOMEWORK: PAGE 98

TAXI

Book Signing TODAY

ISLAND FUN

Words in Action

1. Look at the list. Which are the five most difficult jobs? Why? Which are the five easiest? Why?

2. Look at the list. Which people use vehicles in their jobs? What vehicles do they use? Which people use equipment in their jobs? What equipment do they use?

Working

Words in Context

Needed: Office Assistant

Can you answer phones, **take** messages, **schedule** appointments, and **file**? Can you **use** a computer and a fax machine? Can you **type** 50 words per minute? You may be the right person for this job. Call 555-9389 to schedule an appointment for an interview.

1 cook
2 examine
3 speak
4 arrest
5 open mail
6 load
7 deliver
8 type

9 take care of
10 act / perform
11 sing
12 take a message
13 hire
14 sell
15 repair / fix
16 plan

17 staple

18 manage

19 design

20 make copies

21 use a computer

22 call in sick

23 manufacture

24 file

25 drive

26 make a decision

...and then...

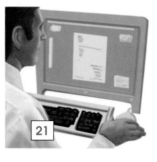

Word Partnerships

attend	a weekly	meeting
	a company	
take	a short	break
	a coffee	
make	a tough	decision
	an easy	
	a good	
	a bad	

Words in Action

1. Which of the things on the list can you do?
2. Choose five verbs on the list. Look at the jobs on pages 146–149. Can you find one or more jobs that match the verb?

Farm

Words in Context

Jimmy Carter was the 39th president of the U.S. He grew up on a **farm** full of animals. There were **dogs, turkeys, horses,** and **cows** on the farm. Carter did many jobs around the farm. He **milked** the cows each day after school. He also **picked** cotton and peanuts in the **fields.**

1 an orchard	10 soil	20 a rooster
2 a silo	11 a crop	21 a goat
3 a barn	12 a scarecrow	22 a horse
4 a tractor	13 hay	23 a sheep
5 a plow	14 a farmer	24 a donkey
6 a farmworker / a farmhand	15 a farmhouse	25 a pig
7 a bull	16 a dog	26 a cow
8 a vineyard	17 a cat	27 a turkey
9 a field	18 a rabbit	28 a chicken
	19 a goose	

Verbs

29 plant

30 water

31 pick

32 milk

33 feed

Animal	Baby Animal
dog	puppy
cat	kitten
chicken	chick
pig	piglet
sheep	lamb
cow	calf
goat	kid

Words in Action

1. Study the word list for three minutes. Then close your book. Write down as many of the words as you can remember. Write each word under one of these categories: *People and animals on a farm, Things on a farm, Places on a farm.*

2. Choose a word and draw a picture of it on the board. The first classmate to guess the word gets a point and draws the next picture on the board.

Office

Words in Context

Offices are very different today than they were 100 years ago. Back then there were no **computers, fax machines,** or **photocopiers.** People used **typewriters** to write letters. However, some things are the same. Most offices still have **file cabinets** and use supplies like **staplers, paper clips,** and **rubber bands.**

Employee of the Month

1

2

3

4

5

6

7

8

9

10

11

12

13

14

15

16

17

JOHN LOPEZ
45 Lawrence Street • Brooklyn, New York 11203 • (718) 555-0303

Executive Assistant

QUALIFICATIONS

• A highly organized and detail-oriented Executive Assistant providing skillful administrative support.
• Able to prioritize tasks and achieve goals.
• A self-motivated professional.
• Excellent research and writing skills.
Computer skills include: MS Word, PowerPoint, Excel

EXPERIENCE

KEMCORP, New York, N.Y.

• Executive Assistant to the CEO, 2003-present
• Coordinated conference calls.
• Created effective filing systems, including quick indexing, fili...
• Conducted exhaustive research on competitors.
Updated and maintained CEO's calendar.
...eduled appointments with important clients an...
... systems and procedures which o...

1 a typewriter

2 a binder

3 a fax machine

4 a (photo)copier / a copy machine

5 a (photo)copy

6 an office manager

7 a desk

8 a computer

9 tape

10 a stapler

11 a calculator

12 a telephone

13 letterhead

14 an appointment book / a date book

15 a business card file

16 a (paper) shredder

17 a resume

18 a file cabinet

19 an office assistant / a secretary

20 a (file) folder

21 an (electric) pencil sharpener

22 a supply cabinet

23 a thumbtack

24 a rubber band

25 glue

26 sticky notes

27 staples

28 correction fluid

29 a paper clip

30 a hole punch

31 a pad

32 a label

Word Partnerships

double sided packing	tape
hook up turn on turn off	a fax machine a computer

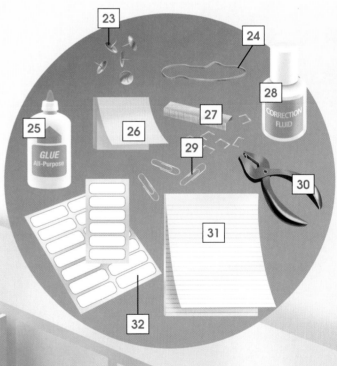

Words in Action

1. Which items on the list do you have at home?

2. Work with a partner. One student describes an office item. The other student guesses the item.
   - Student A: *You use this to add numbers.*
   - Student B: *A calculator.*

Factory

1 a designer
2 a front office
3 an assembly line
4 a worker
5 a robot
6 a conveyor belt
7 a packer
8 a hard hat
9 a supervisor

Words in Context

Making a chair is a process. There are many steps. The **designer** creates a design. **Parts** for the chair arrive at the **factory**'s **loading dock.** Then **assembly line workers** put the chair together. It travels down a **conveyor belt** and gets a new part at each area. At the end of the assembly line, **packers** put the chair into a box. It goes into a **warehouse.** Then a **shipping clerk** sends it to a store near you!

PARTS

FRONT OFFICE

30 biohazard

31 electrical hazard

32 explosive materials

33 flammable materials

34 poisonous materials

35 radioactive materials

10 a forklift

11 a time card

12 a time clock

13 parts

14 a machine operator

15 a warehouse

16 a shipping clerk

17 a fire extinguisher

18 a loading dock

19 a hand truck / a dolly

20 a hairnet

21 a safety visor

22 a respirator

23 safety goggles

24 earplugs

25 safety glasses

26 a particle mask

27 a safety vest

28 safety boots

29 safety earmuffs

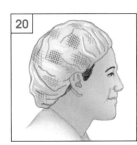

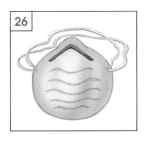

Word Partnerships

a factory	worker
an assembly line	
a forklift	operator
a shift	supervisor
	worker
punch	a time card

Words in Action

1. Make a list of the people in this factory. Which job is the most interesting to you? Which is the least interesting? Why?

2. What part of the body do each of these pieces of safety equipment protect: earplugs, a hard hat, safety boots, safety goggles, a safety visor, safety earmuffs, safety glasses, a particle mask, a hairnet.

Hotel

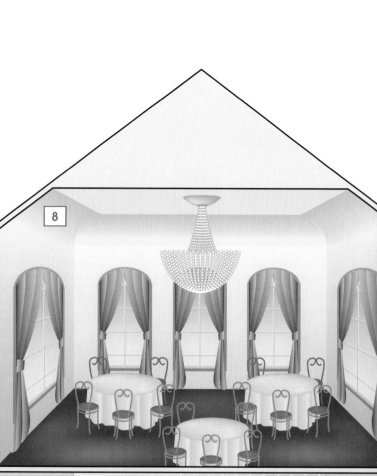

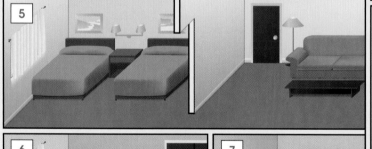

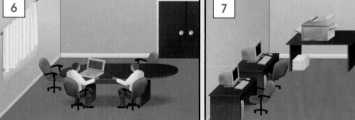

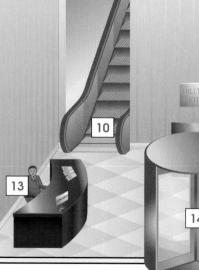

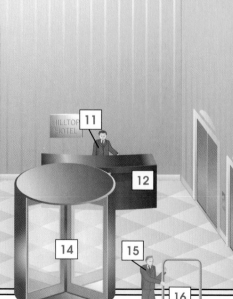

Verbs

24 make a reservation

25 check in

26 order room service

27 check out

1 a housekeeper
2 a housekeeping cart
3 room service
4 a (hotel) guest
5 a suite
6 a meeting room
7 a business center
8 a ballroom
9 a lobby
10 an escalator
11 a desk clerk

12 a registration desk
13 a concierge
14 a revolving door
15 a bellhop
16 a luggage cart
17 a (double) room
18 a (single) room
19 a fitness center
20 a sauna
21 a (swimming) pool
22 a gift shop
23 valet parking

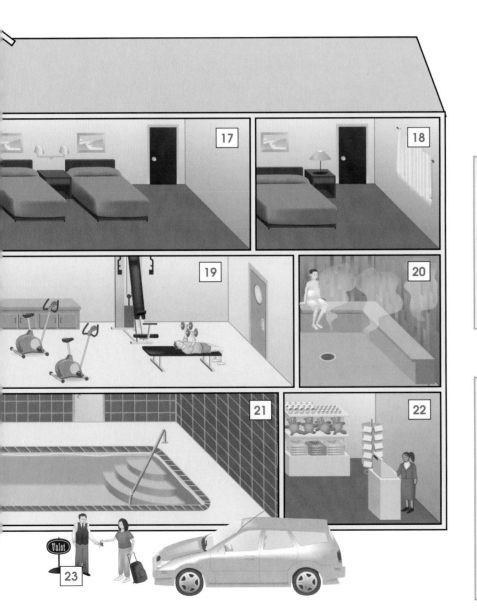

Word Partnerships

a luxury	hotel
a budget	
room	rates
an indoor	(swimming) pool
an outdoor	
a heated	

Words in Action

1. Make three lists: *People in a Hotel, Places in a Hotel,* and *Things in a Hotel.*

2. Role-play with a partner. One of you is the desk clerk at a hotel. The other is calling with questions about the hotel.
   - Student A: *How much is a double room?*
   - Student B: *It's $50 a night for a double.*
   - Student A: *Is there a swimming pool?*

Tools and Supplies 1

Words in Context

I go to hardware stores a lot because I work in construction. I keep my **wrench,** my **hammer,** and my **screwdriver** in my **tool belt.** Those are the **tools** I use the most.

Hand Tools

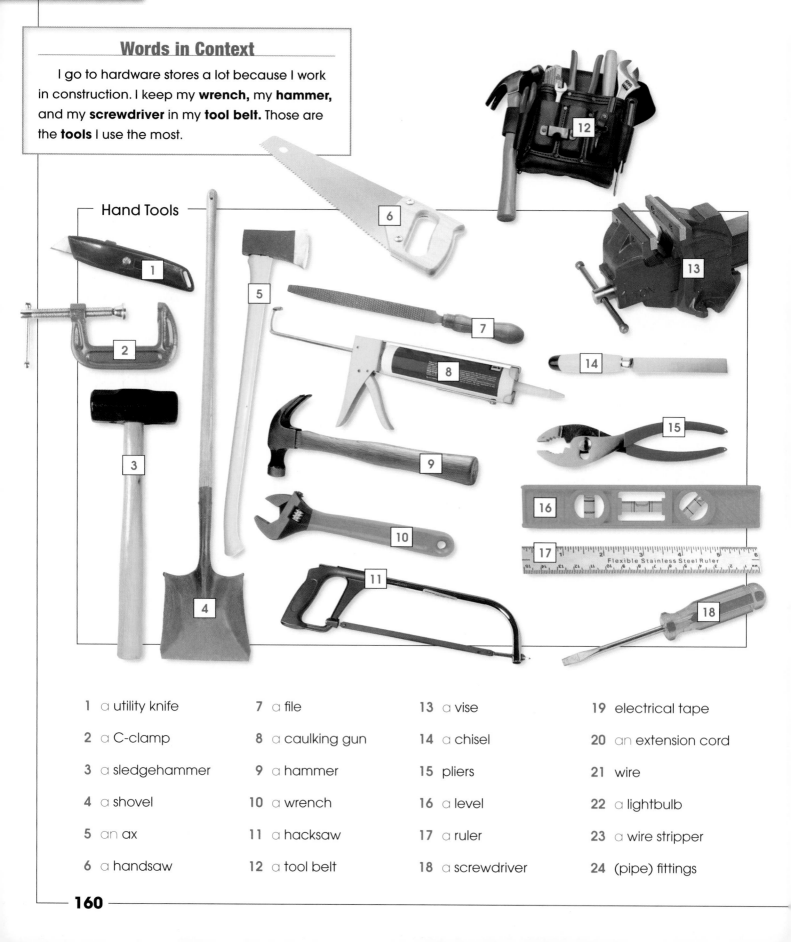

1 a utility knife	7 a file	13 a vise	19 electrical tape
2 a C-clamp	8 a caulking gun	14 a chisel	20 an extension cord
3 a sledgehammer	9 a hammer	15 pliers	21 wire
4 a shovel	10 a wrench	16 a level	22 a lightbulb
5 an ax	11 a hacksaw	17 a ruler	23 a wire stripper
6 a handsaw	12 a tool belt	18 a screwdriver	24 (pipe) fittings

Electrical

Plumbing

Power Tools

25 a pipe wrench

26 a pipe

27 a router

28 a drill

29 a drill bit

30 a blade

31 a circular saw

32 a power sander

Words in Action

1. Which items on the list have you used? What job did you do with each item?

2. Which tools would you use to:
   - build a bookcase?
   - wire a house?
   - install a sink?

Tools and Supplies 2

Words in Context

How to Hang a Picture on a Wall

- With a **tape measure** or ruler, measure 66 to 68 **inches** above the floor.

- Put a small piece of **masking tape** on the wall.

- Put a **nail** through a picture **hook,** and pound it in through the masking tape.

- Hang your picture.

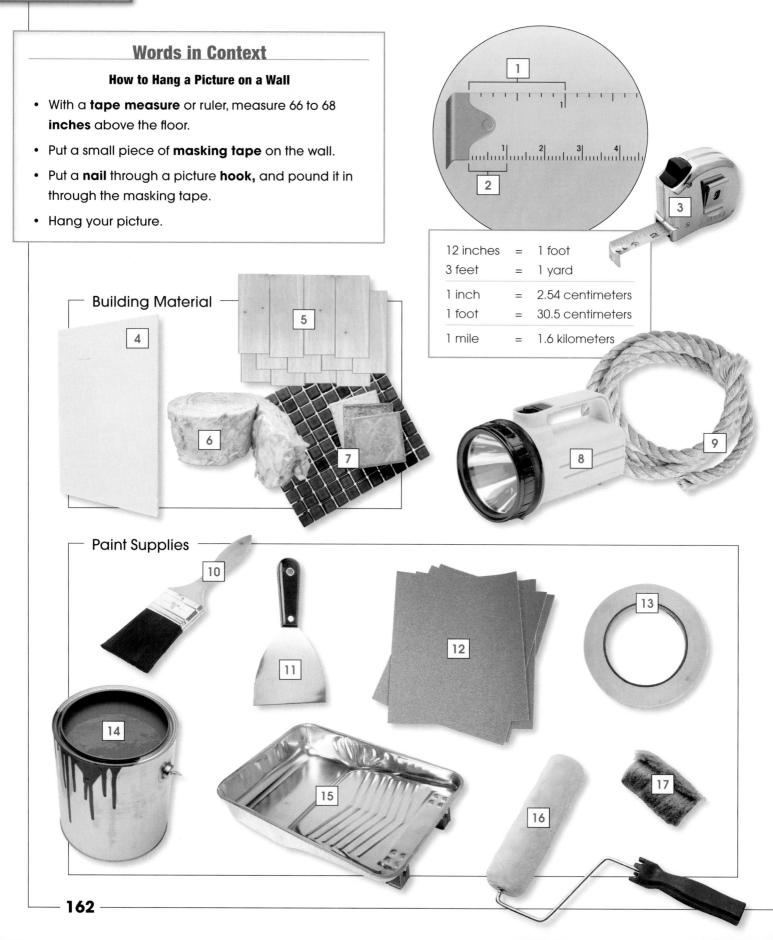

12 inches	=	1 foot
3 feet	=	1 yard
1 inch	=	2.54 centimeters
1 foot	=	30.5 centimeters
1 mile	=	1.6 kilometers

Building Material

Paint Supplies

Hardware

18
19
20
21
22
23
24
25
26
27

Lumber / Wood

28
29
30
31
32
33

1 an inch

2 a centimeter

3 a tape measure

4 drywall

5 shingles

6 insulation

7 tile

8 a flashlight

9 a rope

10 a paintbrush

11 a scraper

12 sandpaper

13 masking tape

14 paint

15 a paint tray

16 a (paint) roller

17 steel wool

18 an anchor

19 an eye hook

20 a nail

21 a bolt

22 a screw

23 a nut

24 a wing nut

25 a hinge

26 a washer

27 a hook

28 plywood

29 molding

30 board lumber

31 duct tape

32 a chain

33 a battery

34 a padlock

Word Partnerships

a hardware	store
	section
a sheet of	plywood
	drywall
spray	paint
latex	
acrylic	

Words in Action

1. Name one of the items on the list, then think of as many uses for the item as you can.

2. Imagine you need to paint some windows in an old house. Which items will you need to prepare the windows and paint them?

Drill, Sand, Paint

Words in Context

In 1980, Edouard Arsenault, a Canadian fisherman, began to make buildings with old glass bottles. He used thousands of bottles. He **mixed** cement. Then, instead of **laying** bricks, he laid rows of bottles in the wet cement. After he **put up** the glass walls, he **installed** skylights. Many people visit these buildings each year.

Word Partnerships

paint	a wall
	a room
	a house
install	a phone line
	a water heater
shovel	gravel
	snow

1 put up drywall

2 plaster a wall

3 paint a wall

4 drill a hole

5 lay bricks

6 pull a rope

7 pour concrete

8 wire a house

9 hammer a nail

10 saw wood

11 measure

12 weld

13 install a window

14 climb a ladder

15 operate a backhoe

16 tear down a wall

17 read blueprints

18 carry a bag

19 shovel sand

20 push a wheelbarrow

21 cut a pipe

22 dig a trench

23 plane wood

24 glue wood

25 sand wood

Words in Action

1. Check off the things on the list you have done.

2. Pretend to be doing one of the actions on the word list. Your partner will guess what you are doing.

Weather

Words in Context

Today's **weather:**

Don't expect **sunshine** today. The morning will be **cold** and **windy** with a good chance of **rain.** This afternoon the temperature will drop, and we will see five to seven inches of **snow** tonight!

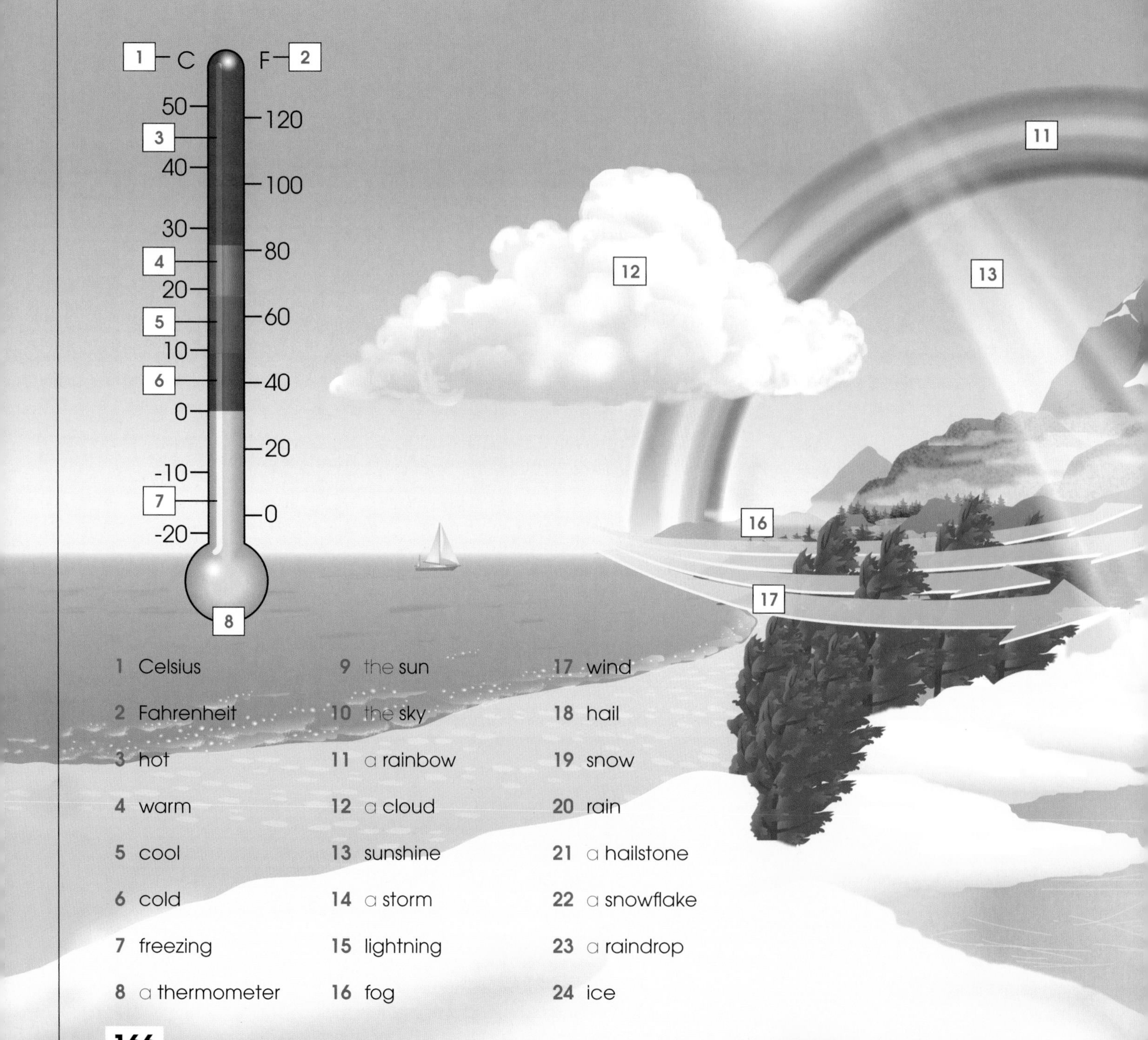

1 Celsius
2 Fahrenheit
3 hot
4 warm
5 cool
6 cold
7 freezing
8 a thermometer
9 the sun
10 the sky
11 a rainbow
12 a cloud
13 sunshine
14 a storm
15 lightning
16 fog
17 wind
18 hail
19 snow
20 rain
21 a hailstone
22 a snowflake
23 a raindrop
24 ice

25 It's sunny.

26 It's cloudy.

27 It's windy.

28 It's snowing.

29 It's foggy.

30 It's raining.

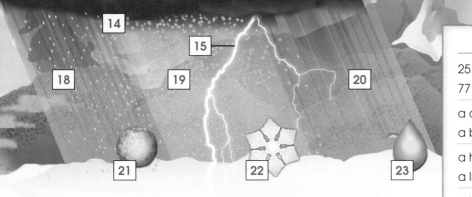

Word Partnerships

25	degrees	Celsius
77		Fahrenheit
a cold	wind	
a bitter		
a heavy	rain	
a light		
a blue	sky	
a gray		
a cloudless		

Words in Action

1. Describe the weather today. Then describe yesterday's weather.
   - *It's rainy and cool today. Yesterday was sunny and warm.*

2. What is your favorite kind of weather? Why?
   - *I like sunny weather because I can go to the beach.*

The Earth's Surface

1

3

2

4

5

9

6

7

8

16

20

19

18

17

1 a peak
2 a mountain
3 a volcano
4 a glacier
5 a valley
6 a stream
7 a lake
8 an island
9 a waterfall

10 a crater
11 a desert
12 a plateau
13 a canyon
14 a cave
15 a mesa
16 a forest
17 a peninsula
18 a shore

19 the mouth of the river
20 a riverbank
21 a river
22 a hill
23 a beach

24 an ocean
25 a bay
26 plains
27 a cliff

Word Partnerships

a sandy a rocky	beach
a deep a shallow	river
a mountain	peak range
an active	volcano
a steep	hill

Words in Action

1. Plan a vacation. Pick five things from the list that you want to see on your vacation. Write them down, then share your list with a classmate.

2. Make lists of all of the oceans, rivers, and lakes you know. Use a map to add more to your list. Share your list with a classmate.

Energy, Pollution, and Natural Disasters

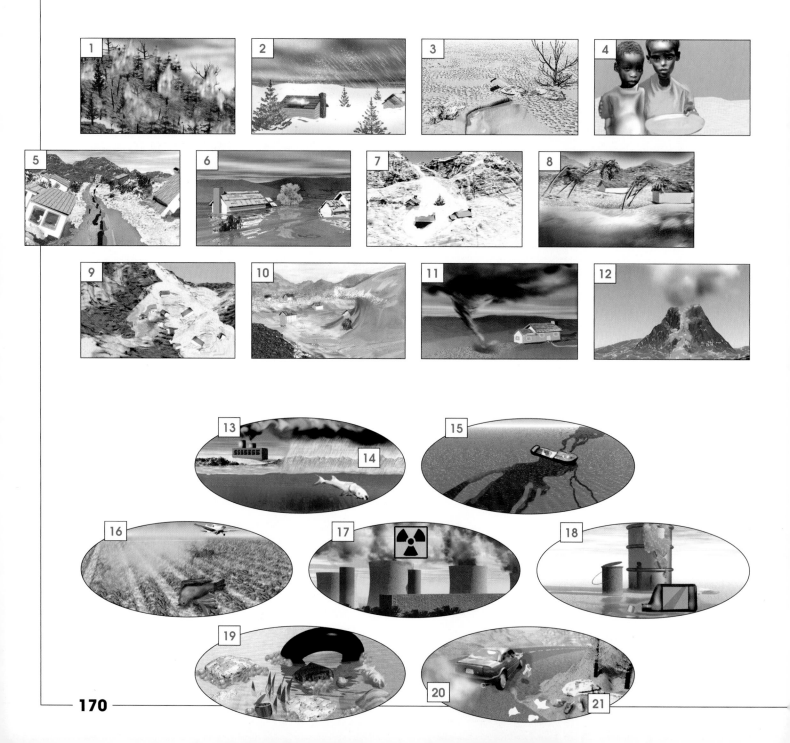

Natural Disasters

1 a forest fire

2 a blizzard

3 a drought

4 a famine

5 an earthquake

6 a flood

7 an avalanche

8 a hurricane

9 a mudslide

10 a tsunami / a tidal wave

11 a tornado

12 a volcanic eruption

Pollution

13 air pollution / smog

14 acid rain

15 an oil spill

16 pesticide poisoning

17 radiation

18 hazardous waste

19 water pollution

20 automobile exhaust

21 litter

Energy

22 natural gas

23 oil / petroleum

24 wind

25 geothermal energy

26 coal

27 solar energy

28 nuclear energy

29 hydroelectric power

Word Partnerships

a long	drought
a severe	
a flash	flood
a minor	earthquake
a major	
environmental	disasters
	pollution

Words in Action

1. Work with a group. Choose two or three natural disasters. In what parts of the world has each disaster happened? Make a list for each disaster.

2. Which kind of energy source do you use to heat your home? Which do you use to cook? Which do you use to dry your clothes? Discuss with a group.

The United States and Canada

Words in Context

There are fifty states in the **United States.** The capital is **Washington, D.C.** The U.S. city with the most people is **New York City.** **Canada** is much larger than the U.S., but it has far fewer people. The capital of Canada is **Ottawa** and the city with the most people is **Toronto.**

Regions of Canada

1 Northern Canada
2 British Columbia
3 the Prairie Provinces
4 Ontario
5 Quebec
6 the Atlantic Provinces

Regions of the United States

7 the West Coast
8 the Rocky Mountain States
9 the Midwest
10 the Mid-Atlantic States
11 New England
12 the Southwest
13 the South

ARCTIC OCEAN

Yukon
Whitehorse ★

British Columbia
2

Alberta
Edmonton ★

Saskatchewan
3

Northwest Territories
Yellowknife ★

1

Nunavut

Iqaluit ★

Manitoba

Ontario
4

Québec
5

Newfoundland & Labrador
6

St. John's ★

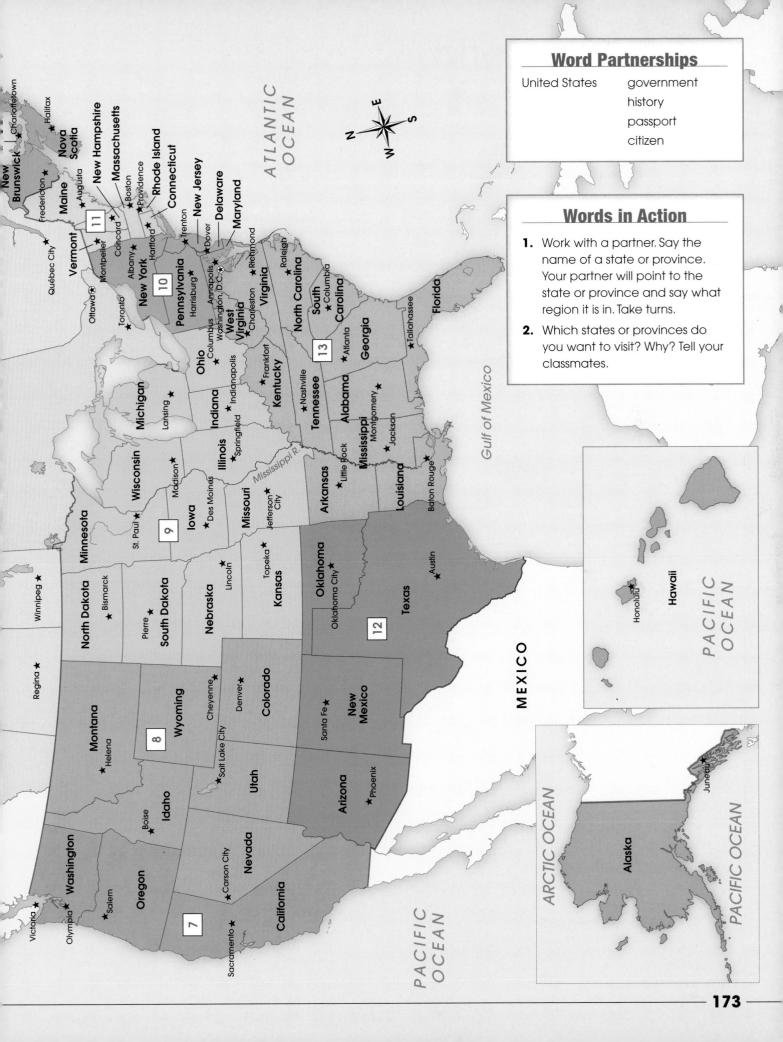

Word Partnerships

United States	government
	history
	passport
	citizen

Words in Action

1. Work with a partner. Say the name of a state or province. Your partner will point to the state or province and say what region it is in. Take turns.

2. Which states or provinces do you want to visit? Why? Tell your classmates.

ATLANTIC OCEAN

New Brunswick
Charlottetown
Halifax
Nova Scotia
Fredericton
Maine
New Hampshire
Massachusetts
Augusta
Concord
Boston
Providence
Rhode Island
Connecticut
New Jersey
Delaware
Maryland
Trenton
Dover
Hartford
Richmond
Raleigh
Québec City
Vermont
Montpelier
Albany
New York
11
10
Ottawa
Toronto
Pennsylvania
Harrisburg
Annapolis
Washington, D.C.
West Virginia
Charleston
Virginia
North Carolina
Columbia
South Carolina
Florida
Columbus
Ohio
Frankfort
Kentucky
Nashville
Atlanta
13
Georgia
Tallahassee
Michigan
Lansing
Indiana
Indianapolis
Springfield
Tennessee
Alabama
Montgomery
Gulf of Mexico
Wisconsin
Madison
Illinois
Mississippi R.
Missouri
Jefferson City
Arkansas
Little Rock
Mississippi
Jackson
Louisiana
Baton Rouge
Minnesota
St. Paul
Iowa
Des Moines
9
Winnipeg
North Dakota
Bismarck
South Dakota
Pierre
Nebraska
Lincoln
Topeka
Kansas
Oklahoma
Oklahoma City
Austin
Texas
MEXICO
Regina
Montana
Helena
Wyoming
Cheyenne
Denver
Colorado
Santa Fe
New Mexico
12
8
Idaho
Boise
Salt Lake City
Utah
Arizona
Phoenix
Washington
Olympia
Salem
Oregon
Nevada
Carson City
Sacramento
California
7
Victoria

PACIFIC OCEAN

ARCTIC OCEAN

Alaska
Juneau

PACIFIC OCEAN

Hawaii
Honolulu
PACIFIC OCEAN

173

The World

Words in Context

There are seven **continents** and almost 200 countries in the **world**. **Russia** and **Canada** are the biggest countries. **China** and **India** are the countries with the most people.

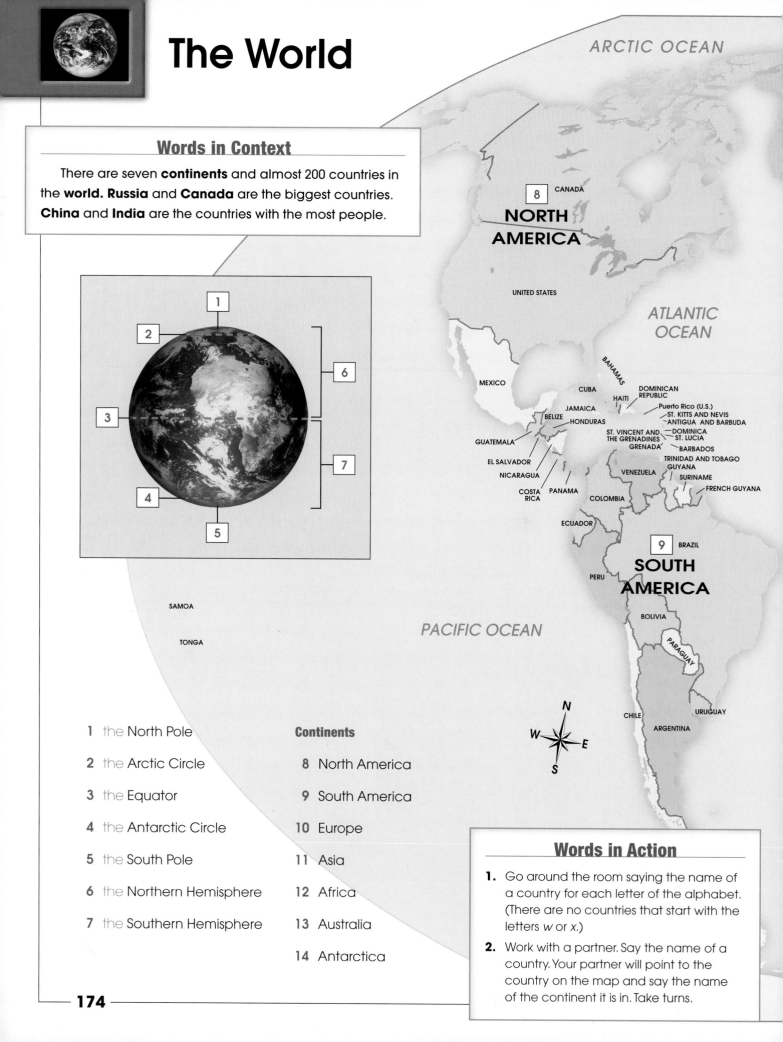

NORTH AMERICA

8 CANADA

UNITED STATES

ATLANTIC OCEAN

MEXICO

BAHAMAS

CUBA

HAITI

DOMINICAN REPUBLIC

Puerto Rico (U.S.)

ST. KITTS AND NEVIS

ANTIGUA AND BARBUDA

JAMAICA

BELIZE

HONDURAS

GUATEMALA

ST. VINCENT AND THE GRENADINES

DOMINICA

ST. LUCIA

GRENADA

BARBADOS

EL SALVADOR

TRINIDAD AND TOBAGO

GUYANA

NICARAGUA

VENEZUELA

SURINAME

FRENCH GUYANA

COSTA RICA

PANAMA

COLOMBIA

ECUADOR

9 BRAZIL

SOUTH AMERICA

PERU

SAMOA

PACIFIC OCEAN

TONGA

BOLIVIA

PARAGUAY

N

W E

S

CHILE

URUGUAY

ARGENTINA

1 the North Pole

2 the Arctic Circle

3 the Equator

4 the Antarctic Circle

5 the South Pole

6 the Northern Hemisphere

7 the Southern Hemisphere

Continents

8 North America

9 South America

10 Europe

11 Asia

12 Africa

13 Australia

14 Antarctica

Words in Action

1. Go around the room saying the name of a country for each letter of the alphabet. (There are no countries that start with the letters *w* or *x*.)

2. Work with a partner. Say the name of a country. Your partner will point to the country on the map and say the name of the continent it is in. Take turns.

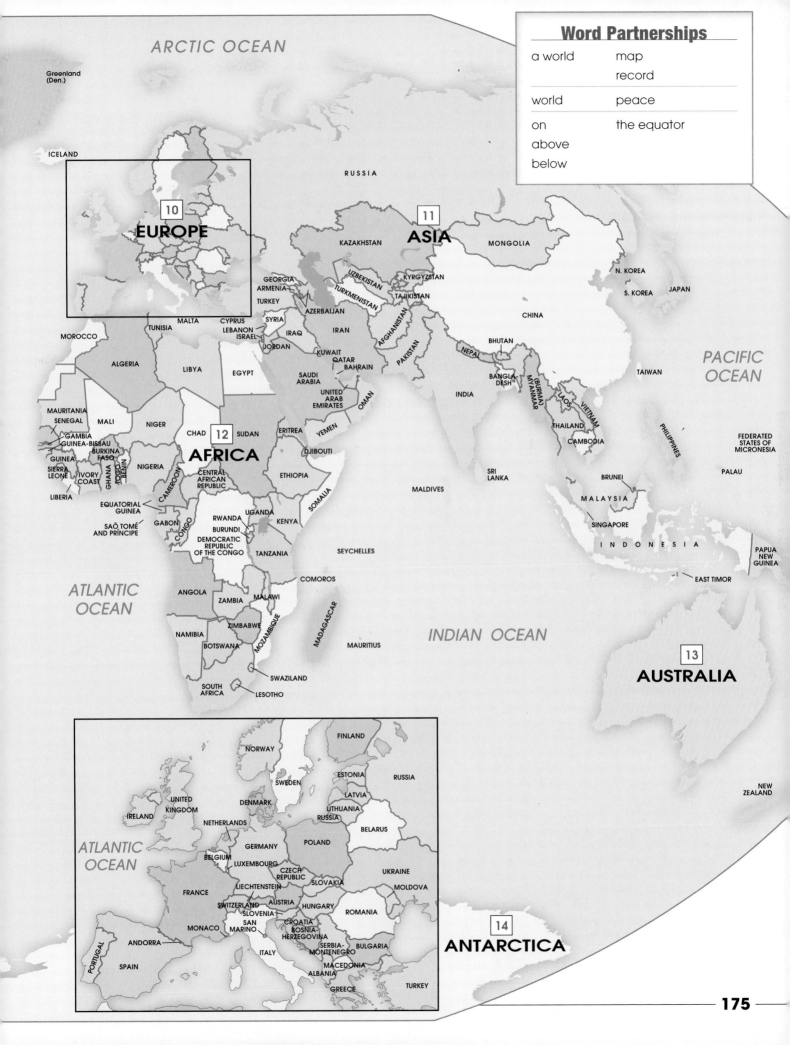

ARCTIC OCEAN

Greenland
(Den.)

ICELAND

Word Partnerships

a world	map
	record
world	peace
on	the equator
above	
below	

RUSSIA

10

EUROPE

11

ASIA

KAZAKHSTAN

MONGOLIA

N. KOREA

GEORGIA
ARMENIA
TURKEY

UZBEKISTAN   KYRGYZSTAN

TURKMENISTAN   TAJIKISTAN

S. KOREA   JAPAN

MALTA
CYPRUS
LEBANON
ISRAEL

AZERBAIJAN

CHINA

TAIWAN

PACIFIC
OCEAN

TUNISIA

MOROCCO

SYRIA
IRAQ

JORDAN

IRAN

AFGHANISTAN

PAKISTAN

NEPAL

BHUTAN

ALGERIA

LIBYA

EGYPT

KUWAIT
QATAR
BAHRAIN

SAUDI
ARABIA

UNITED
ARAB
EMIRATES

OMAN

INDIA

BANGLA-
DESH

(BURMA)
MYANMAR

LAOS

VIETNAM

MAURITANIA

SENEGAL

MALI

NIGER

CHAD

12

SUDAN

ERITREA

YEMEN

THAILAND

CAMBODIA

PHILIPPINES

FEDERATED
STATES OF
MICRONESIA

GAMBIA
GUINEA-BISSAU

GUINEA

SIERRA
LEONE

LIBERIA

BURKINA
FASO

NIGERIA

AFRICA

DJIBOUTI

CENTRAL
AFRICAN
REPUBLIC

ETHIOPIA

SOMALIA

SRI
LANKA

MALDIVES

BRUNEI

PALAU

IVORY
COAST

GHANA
TOGO
BENIN

EQUATORIAL
GUINEA

CAMEROON

MALAYSIA

SAÕ TOMÉ
AND PRÍNCIPE

GABON

CONGO

RWANDA

UGANDA

BURUNDI

DEMOCRATIC
REPUBLIC
OF THE CONGO

KENYA

TANZANIA

SEYCHELLES

SINGAPORE

INDONESIA

PAPUA
NEW
GUINEA

EAST TIMOR

ATLANTIC
OCEAN

ANGOLA

ZAMBIA

MALAWI

COMOROS

MADAGASCAR

INDIAN OCEAN

13

NAMIBIA

ZIMBABWE

BOTSWANA

MOZAMBIQUE

MAURITIUS

AUSTRALIA

SOUTH
AFRICA

SWAZILAND

LESOTHO

NEW
ZEALAND

FINLAND

NORWAY

SWEDEN

ESTONIA

RUSSIA

UNITED
KINGDOM

DENMARK

LATVIA

LITHUANIA

IRELAND

NETHERLANDS

RUSSIA

BELARUS

ATLANTIC
OCEAN

BELGIUM

GERMANY

LUXEMBOURG

POLAND

UKRAINE

CZECH
REPUBLIC

SLOVAKIA

FRANCE

LIECHTENSTEIN

MOLDOVA

SWITZERLAND

AUSTRIA

HUNGARY

SLOVENIA

MONACO

SAN
MARINO

CROATIA
BOSNIA-
HERZEGOVINA

ROMANIA

14

ANDORRA

PORTUGAL

ITALY

SERBIA-
MONTENEGRO

BULGARIA

ANTARCTICA

SPAIN

MACEDONIA

ALBANIA

GREECE

TURKEY

The Universe

Words in Context

The first **satellite** went into **space** in 1957. The first human went into space in 1961. In 1969 an **astronaut** walked on the **moon** for the first time. Today some astronauts even live on a **space station** for a few months at a time!

1 a space station

2 a constellation

3 a star

4 a rocket

5 an eclipse

6 an orbit

7 a galaxy

8 an observatory

9 a telescope

10 an astronomer

11 space

12 the moon

13 a satellite

14 an astronaut

15 Earth's atmosphere

16 a meteor

17 a space shuttle

18 the sun

19 a comet

The Planets

20 Pluto

21 Neptune

22 Uranus

23 Saturn

24 Jupiter

25 Mars

26 Earth

27 Venus

28 Mercury

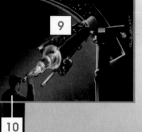

29 a new moon

30 a crescent moon

31 a quarter moon

32 a full moon

Word Partnerships

space	travel
	exploration
a distant	star
a shooting	
a bright	
a solar	eclipse
a lunar	

Words in Action

1. Imagine you are an astronaut. You can go to any one place in the solar system. Where will you go? Why? Share your answer with the class.

2. Look at the sky tonight and report back to your class. Was it a new moon, a crescent moon, a quarter moon, or a full moon? Does everyone in the class agree?

Garden

3

1

2

4

14

16

15

17

10

11

13

12

18

Parts of a Tree

Parts of a Flower

25

26

21

22

19

20

23

24

178

1. a pine (tree)
2. a willow (tree)
3. a birch (tree)
4. a maple (tree)
5. an oak (tree)
6. an elm (tree)
7. a lilac bush
8. a greenhouse
9. a pinecone
10. a branch
11. a trunk

12. roots
13. a leaf
14. a flower
15. a stem
16. a petal
17. a bud
18. a bulb
19. irises
20. lilies
21. chrysanthemums
22. daffodils

23. violets
24. a seed
25. tulips
26. marigolds
27. ivy
28. roses
29. sunflowers
30. geraniums
31. daisies
32. poppies

Word Partnerships

a shade	tree
an evergreen	
send	flowers
give	
get / receive	
a bouquet of	roses
a dozen	
long-stem	

Words in Action

1. Which of the flowers and trees grow in your area? Make a list with your class.

2. Describe a flower or tree to a partner. Your partner will guess the flower or tree. Take turns.
   - Student A: *It has a yellow center and white petals. It doesn't really have a smell.*
   - Student B: *It's a daisy.*

Desert

1 a hawk	7 a palm tree	13 a rat	**Insects / Bugs**
2 an owl	8 a camel	14 a snake	18 a spider
3 a boulder	9 a vulture	15 an oasis	19 a grasshopper
4 a coyote	10 a lizard	16 a cactus	20 a fly
5 a mountain lion	11 a rock	17 a pebble	21 a moth
6 a sand dune	12 a tortoise		22 a cricket
			23 a scorpion
			24 an ant

Words in Action

1. One student chooses a word from the word list. The other students ask "Yes / No" questions to gather information and try to guess the word.
   - Student A: *Is it an animal?*
     Student B: *No.*
   - Student C: *Is it an insect?*
     Student B: *Yes.*
   - Student D: *Does it have wings?*
     Student B: *Yes.*
   - Student D: *Is it a fly?*
     Student B: *Yes!*

2. Imagine you are taking a trip to the desert. What things do you want to see? Discuss this with your class.

Rain Forest

Words in Context

Many plants and animals live in **rain forests.** Colorful **parrots** and playful **monkeys** live there. Beautiful **orchids** and long **vines** grow there. At night, **tigers** and **panthers** hunt in the rain forest.

1 a parakeet
2 a vine
3 a chimpanzee
4 a bat
5 a parrot
6 a monkey
7 a gorilla
8 a peacock
9 a tiger
10 a hummingbird
11 an orchid
12 a frog
13 an orangutan

14 an aardvark
15 a flamingo
16 a fern
17 a panther
18 an alligator
19 a crocodile
20 a caterpillar
21 a butterfly
22 a snail
23 a wasp
24 a beetle
25 a tarantula

Word Partnerships

frogs	hop
wasps	sting
tigers	leap
monkeys	swing

182

Verbs

26 swing

27 hop

28 hang

Words in Action

1. Work with a partner. Put the words into groups of plants, animals, and insects.

2. Choose one of the animals on the list that makes a noise. Make that animal's noise. Your partner will guess the animal. Take turns.

Grasslands

Animals in the **grasslands** have different sources of food. **Giraffes** and **elephants** graze on the tallest trees. **Buffalo** and **gazelles** graze on grasses. The large cats, like **lions, leopards,** and **cheetahs,** feed on other animals.

1

2

5

6

7

8

10

11

12

13

14

15

16

20

21

22

23

24

25

1	a bee	16	a shrub / a bush
2	a fossil	17	a buffalo
3	a koala	18	a sparrow
4	a kangaroo	19	a gopher
5	a hyena	20	a lion
6	a giraffe	21	an antler
7	a hippopotamus	22	a hoof
8	a rhinoceros	23	a horn
9	an antelope	24	a tusk
10	an elephant	25	a trunk
11	a leopard	26	a mane
12	a zebra	27	a paw
13	a cheetah	28	fur
14	an ostrich	29	a tail
15	a gazelle		

Word Partnerships

a herd of	antelope
	buffalo
	elephants
lions	roar
bees	buzz
hyenas	laugh

Words in Action

1. Which animals on the list have fur? Which have a tail? Which have paws? Make lists with a partner.

2. Describe an animal to a partner. Your partner says the name and points to the correct picture.
   - Student A: *It's big and it has two horns on its head.*
   - Student B: (pointing to the rhinocerous) *It's a rhinoceros.*

Polar Lands

Words in Context

Many animals live on the ice or in the waters near the North Pole. They stay warm in different ways. The **whale** and the **walrus** have thick layers of body fat. The arctic **fox** and the **polar bear** stay warm in their thick, white fur. Even **moss** finds a way to stay warm. It grows over rocks facing the sun.

Word Partnerships

a humpback	whale
a blue	
a Canada	goose
a wild	
a pack of	wolves
a flock of	birds

186

1 a goose	6 moss	11 a fox	16 whiskers	21 a wing
2 a moose	7 an otter	12 a seal	17 a tusk	22 a claw
3 a reindeer	8 a (polar) bear	13 a penguin	18 a flipper	23 a feather
4 a wolf	9 a (bear) cub	14 a whale	19 a falcon	
5 a (grizzly) bear	10 an iceberg	15 a walrus	20 a beak	

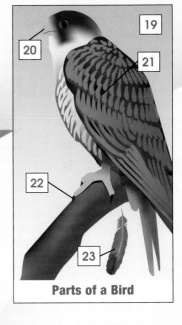

Parts of a Bird

Words in Action

1. Which polar animals eat meat? Which eat plants? Discuss these questions with your classmates.

2. In a group, make one list of the polar animals with wings, a second list of the animals with flippers, and a third list of the animals with claws. Compare lists among groups.

Sea

Words in Context

There are more than 15,000 kinds of **fish** in the **sea.** The largest fish is the **shark.** The great white shark can grow to over 7 meters*. There are also some very fast fish in the sea. For example, the **swordfish** swims at about 90 kilometers** per hour, and the **tuna** swims at about 70 kilometers*** per hour. The slowest fish is the **sea horse.** It only swims about 0.001 kilometers per hour!

* 7 meters = 23.1 feet   ** 90 kilometers = 55.8 miles   *** 70 kilometers = 43.4 miles

Parts of a Fish

Word Partnerships

a school of	fish
a freshwater	
a saltwater	
a sea	turtle
a snapping	
a hammerhead	shark
a great white	

1 a seagull
2 a dolphin
3 a swordfish
4 gills
5 a fin
6 scales
7 a killer whale / an orca
8 a turtle
9 seaweed
10 a tuna
11 a jellyfish
12 a shark
13 a (scuba) diver
14 a sea horse
15 a bass

16 a cod
17 an octopus
18 an eel
19 a squid
20 a stingray
21 a shrimp
22 a sea urchin
23 an angelfish
24 a crab
25 a sea anemone
26 a coral reef
27 a mussel
28 a starfish
29 a sponge
30 a halibut

Words in Action

1. Make a list of all the sea animals you have seen. Then compare your list with your classmates' lists.

2. Study the spread for five minutes. Close your books. With a group, make a list of as many sea animals as you can remember. Take turns describing what each one looks like. You may want to draw pictures on the board.

Woodlands

Words in Context

Woodland animals have many different homes. Some, like **moles** and **rabbits,** live underground. **Cardinals, blue jays,** and other birds make their **nests** in trees. **Squirrels** also live in trees and keep their nuts and berries there.

1 a robin
2 a cardinal
3 a nest
4 a blue jay
5 an eagle
6 a bobcat
7 an opossum
8 a squirrel
9 a deer
10 a groundhog
11 a porcupine
12 a turkey
13 a woodpecker
14 a duck
15 a beaver

16 a mole
17 a salamander
18 a worm
19 a raccoon
20 a toad
21 a chipmunk
22 a skunk
23 a dragonfly
24 a mosquito
25 a tick
26 a hornet
27 a ladybug
28 a rabbit
29 a mouse

Word Partnerships

as quiet as a mouse

as busy as a beaver

as prickly as a porcupine

as scared as a rabbit

Words in Action

1. What animals live on or near water? What animals live on land? Make lists with a partner.

2. Choose three animals on the list. Write a list of at least three things you know about each of the animals.
   Ducks
   1. They have wings.
   2. They live on water.
   3. Baby ducks follow their mother.

191

Math

Words in Context

You use **math** every day. You use **subtraction** to balance your checkbook. You use **fractions** to cook. You use **addition** to add up the total on a restaurant bill. You may even use **geometry** to decorate your home. Geometry can help you figure out how much wallpaper you need for your walls and how much carpet you need for your floors.

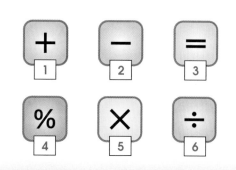

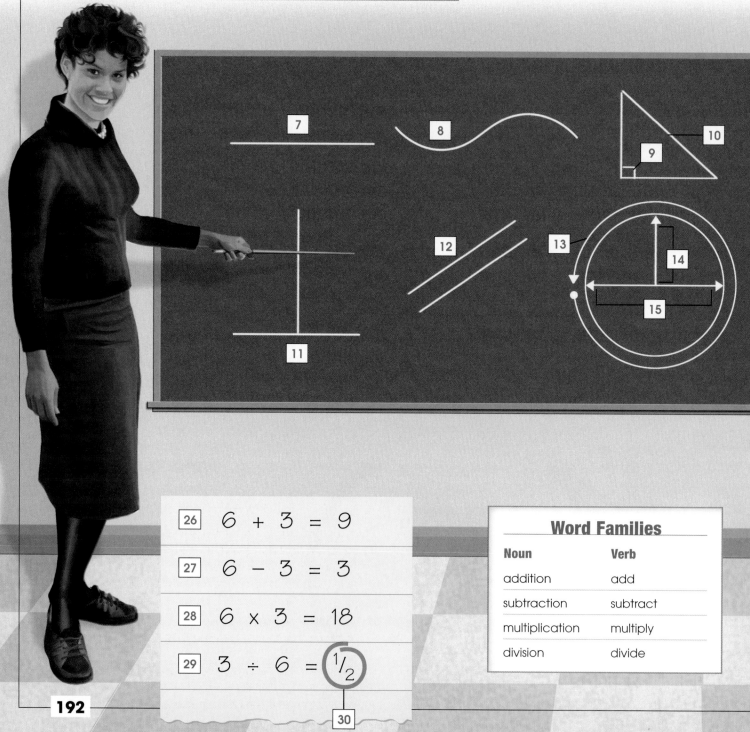

26	$6 + 3 = 9$
27	$6 - 3 = 3$
28	$6 \times 3 = 18$
29	$3 \div 6 = \frac{1}{2}$

Word Families

Noun	Verb
addition	add
subtraction	subtract
multiplication	multiply
division	divide

1 plus

2 minus

3 equals

4 percent

5 multiplied by / times

6 divided by

7 a straight line

8 a curved line

9 an angle

10 a side

11 perpendicular lines

12 parallel lines

13 the circumference

14 the radius

15 the diameter

16 a circle

17 an oval

18 a rectangle

19 a triangle

20 a square

21 a pyramid

22 a cube

23 a sphere

24 a cone

25 a cylinder

26 addition

27 subtraction

28 multiplication

29 division

30 a fraction

31 geometry

32 algebra

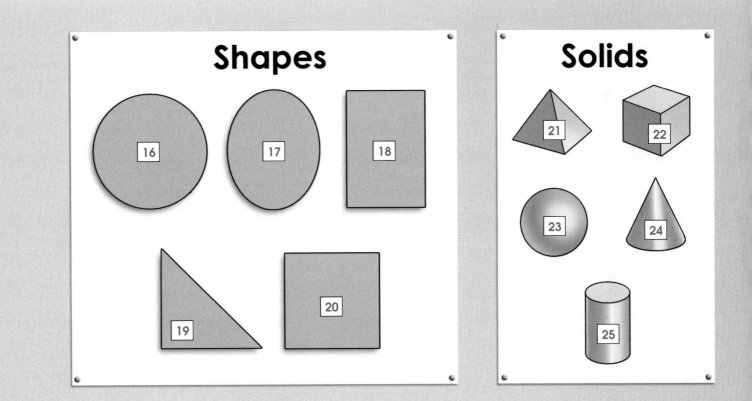

Shapes

Solids

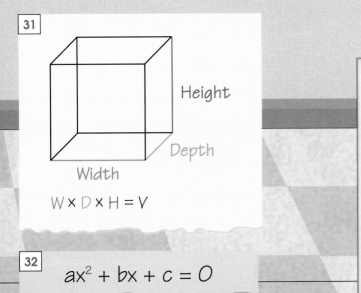

31

Height

Depth

Width

W x D x H = V

32

$$ax^2 + bx + c = 0$$

Words in Action

1. Look around your classroom. Find an example of each of the shapes on the list. Share your ideas with the class.
   - *My desk is a rectangle and the clock is a circle.*
2. Work with a partner. One student writes down a math problem. The other student figures out the answer, then reads the problem and the answer out loud.
   - Student A: (writes: *3 + 3*)
   - Student B: *Three plus three equals six.*

Science

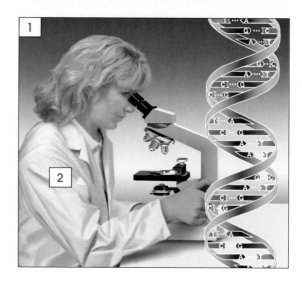

Words in Context

The famous **physicist** Albert Einstein won the Nobel Prize in **Physics** for his ideas about space and time. He is also famous for his **formula** $E = mc^2$. There is even an **element** in the **periodic table** named after Einstein. It's called *einsteinium*.

1 biology
2 a biologist
3 chemistry
4 a chemist
5 physics
6 a physicist
7 a prism
8 forceps
9 a balance
10 a solid
11 a liquid
12 a gas
13 a test tube
14 a Bunsen burner
15 the periodic table
16 an element
17 an atom
18 a molecule
19 a formula
20 a graduated cylinder

21 a dropper
22 a stopper
23 a beaker
24 a flask
25 a microscope
26 a magnifying glass
27 a funnel
28 a slide
29 a petri dish
30 a magnet

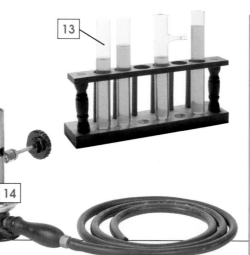

Word Partnerships

a biology	class
a chemistry	lab / laboratory

Word Families

Noun	Adjective
atom	atomic
magnet	magnetic
microscope	microscopic
liquid	liquid
solid	solid

194

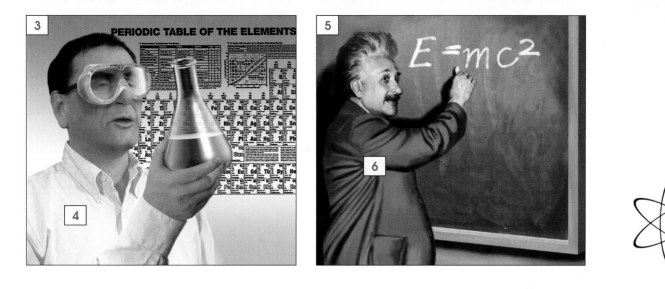

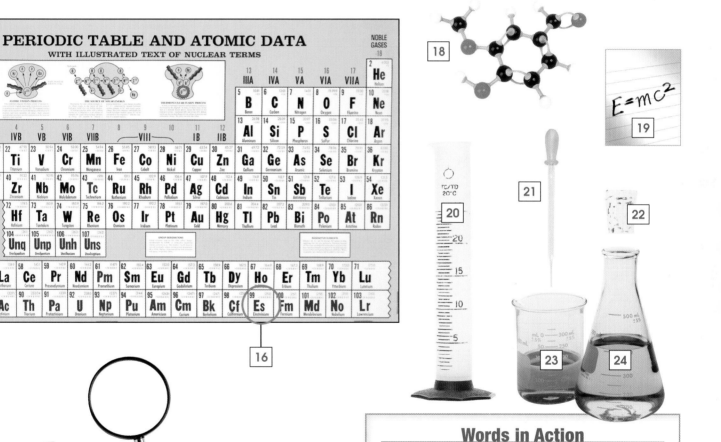

Words in Action

1. Work with a partner. One person describes a laboratory object from the list. The other guesses the object. Take turns.
   - Student A: *You use this to pour liquid into a beaker.*
   - Student B: *A funnel.*

2. Put the items on the word list into three groups: items you find in a physics lab, items you find in a biology lab, and items you find in a chemistry lab. Compare lists with another student. (Note: Some items can be on more than one list.)

Writing

1 a letter	8 a title	14 an apostrophe
2 a word	9 punctuation	15 parentheses
3 a sentence	10 a period	16 quotation marks
4 a paragraph	11 a comma	17 a colon
5 a paper / an essay	12 a question mark	18 a semicolon
6 an indentation	13 an exclamation point / an exclamation mark	19 a hyphen
7 a margin		

Verbs

20 brainstorm ideas

21 write an outline

22 write a draft

23 get feedback

24 edit your essay

25 type your final draft

1 W

2 Writing

3 Writing an essay is a process.

4 Writing an essay is a process. There are four stages to this process: prewriting, drafting, revising, and editing. Each of these stages is an important part in the process that leads a writer to create a well thought out and well organized paper.

5

Megan Purdum
English 1A

6 **8** The Writing Process

7 Writing an essay is a process. There are four stages to this process: prewriting, drafting, revising, and editing. Each of these stages is an important part in the process that leads a writer to create a well thought out and well organized paper.

Prewriting consists of things the writer does before writing a draft of a paper. This is the stage in which the writer gathers and organizes ideas for the paper. This stage can include thinking, talking to others, gathering information, brainstorming, and making an outline of the paper.

In the next stage, the writer writes a draft. While writing a draft, the writer puts ideas into sentences and paragraphs. Each paragraph must have a topic sentence. The topic sentence is what that paragraph is about. The rest of the paragraph should explain and support the topic sentence. It is not important to focus on things like grammar and spelling at this stage.

9

10 •

11 ,

12 ?

13 !

14 '

15 ( )

16 " "

17 :

18 ;

19 -

Word Partnerships

a capital / an uppercase	letter
a lowercase	
a vocabulary	word
a slang	
a one-syllable	
a two-syllable	
a term	paper
a research	

Words in Action

1. Look at a magazine or newspaper article. Find and circle the following:
   - a comma
   - an apostrophe
   - a sentence
   - a paragraph

2. What are the steps in writing a paper? Discuss with a partner.

197

Explore, Rule, Invent

Words in Context

Humans have achieved amazing things. We have **composed** operas and poetry. We have **discovered** cures for diseases. We have **sailed** the world's oceans and **explored** the continents. We have **launched** rockets into space and **reached** the moon.

1 Humans **migrate** from Asia to the Americas.

2 Mesopotamians **produce** the first wheel.

3 The Egyptians **build / construct** pyramids.

4 The Vikings **sail** to present-day Canada.

5 The Chinese **grow** tea.

6 Joan of Arc **defends** France.

7 Montezuma I **rules** the Aztecs.

8 Amerigo Vespucci **explores** the Amazon.

9 Sir Isaac Newton **discovers** gravity.

10 Ludwig van Beethoven **composes** his first symphony.

11 The Suez Canal **opens**.

12 Thomas Edison **invents** the lightbulb.

13 The Wright brothers **fly** the first plane.

14 World War II **ends**.

15 The Soviet Union **launches** the first satellite.

16 Martin Luther King Jr. **wins** the Nobel Peace Prize.

17 Japan **introduces** the high-speed "bullet" train.

18 Apollo 11 astronauts **reach** the moon.

19 The Berlin Wall **falls**.

20 South Africa **elects** Nelson Mandela president.

Word Partnerships	
win	a war
	a contest
compose	a song
	a letter
elect	a prime minister
	a president
	a mayor
build	a road
	a bridge

Words in Action

1. Work with a partner. Cover the sentences. One student points to a picture. The other says the event. Take turns.

2. Work with a partner. One student says one of the verbs from the verb list. The other student uses that verb in a sentence.
   - Student A: *Invent*
   - Student B: *Alexander Graham Bell invented the telephone.*

U.S. Government and Citizenship

Words in Context

The U.S. **government** has three parts. These parts are called *branches.* The executive branch includes the **president** and the **vice president.** The legislative branch includes the **House of Representatives** and the **Senate.** There are 100 **senators** in the Senate and 435 **congressmen** and **congresswomen** in the House of Representatives. The judicial branch includes nine **Supreme Court justices.**

1   a (political) candidate

2   a ballot

3   a voting booth

4   a citizen

5   the U.S. Constitution

6   the Capitol (Building)

7   the White House

8   the Supreme Court

9   a congresswoman / a congressman

10   a senator

11   the president

12   the vice president

13   the justices

We the People of the United States

Article I.

5

Legislative Branch

6

Congress

House of Representatives → Senate

9 10

Executive Branch

7

11 12

Judicial Branch

8

13

Verbs

14 vote

15 obey the law

16 pay taxes

17 serve on a jury

18 protest / demonstrate

19 serve in the military

Word Partnerships

a United States   citizen
                   senator
                   congressman

Words in Action

1. Compare the U.S. government with the government of another country. How are they similar? How are they different?

2. Discuss which branch of the U.S. government you think is most important. Explain your reasons.

Fine Arts

Words in Context

Pablo Picasso is probably the most famous artist of the last 100 years. His **portraits** and **still lifes** hang in the world's great museums. Picasso worked as a **painter, sculptor,** and **potter.** He **painted** with oils and watercolors, and he sculpted in **clay.**

1

2

3

4

5

6

7

8

9

10

11

12

13

14

15

16

17

1	a frame	5	a model	10	paint	15	a mural
2	a still life	6	a palette	11	an easel	16	a sculpture
3	a portrait	7	a painting	12	a canvas	17	a sculptor
4	a landscape	8	a paintbrush	13	a sketchpad	18	pottery
		9	a painter	14	a sketch	19	a potter

15 a mural
16 a sculpture
17 a sculptor
18 pottery
19 a potter
20 a potter's wheel
21 clay
22 a photograph
23 a photographer

Verbs

24 draw

25 paint

26 photograph /
take a photograph

Word Partnerships

modern	art
a work of	

oil	paint
acrylic	
watercolor	

a watercolor	painting
an oil	

Words in Action

1. Work with a group. Make a list of famous artists. Answer the following questions about each:
   - What kind of artist is he/she?
   - What materials did/does this artist use?
   - Do you know the names of any of the artist's works?

2. What is your favorite kind of art? Why? Discuss with a partner.

Performing Arts

1 a ballet
2 a balcony
3 a dancer
4 a mask
5 a costume

6 a stage
7 a conductor
8 an orchestra
9 an audience

Verbs

26 clap / applaud   27 bow

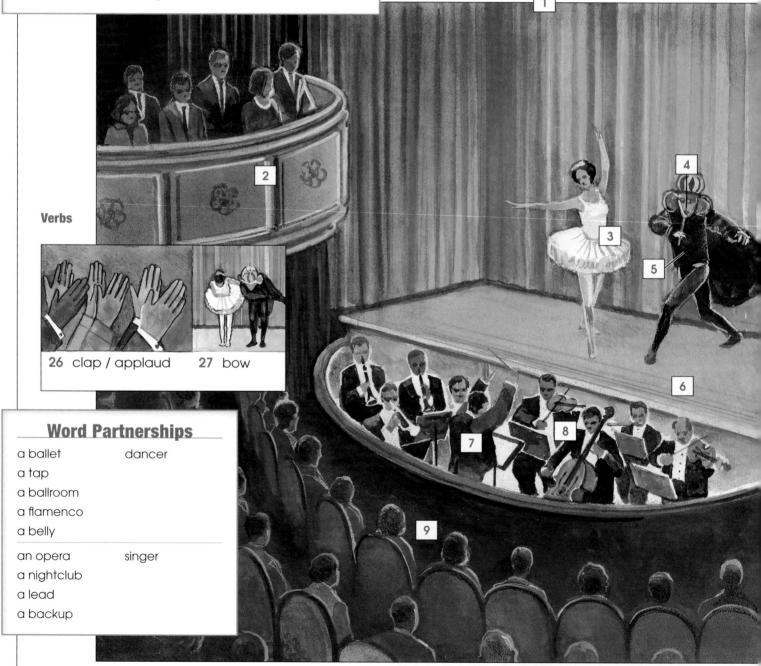

Word Partnerships

a ballet	dancer
a tap	
a ballroom	
a flamenco	
a belly	
an opera	singer
a nightclub	
a lead	
a backup	

10 a (rock) concert	18 an actor
11 a spotlight	19 a set
12 a drummer	20 a seat
13 a microphone	21 an usher
14 a singer	22 a ticket
15 a guitarist	23 a program
16 backup singers	24 a box office
17 a play	25 an opera

Words in Action

1. Have you ever seen a ballet? An opera? A play? Choose your favorite and tell a partner about it.

2. Imagine you are the directors of a new arts center. What kinds of concerts, plays, and other performances will you present this year? Discuss with your group.

Instruments

Words in Context

Percussion instruments are thousands of years old. **Drums** are one of the oldest percussion instruments. They were part of African culture as early as 6000 B.C. The **tambourine** is also thousands of years old. Many countries, from Japan to Morocco to England, use tambourines in their music. Other percussion instruments include **maracas,** from Latin America, and **cymbals,** from China.

Word Partnerships

play	an instrument
tune	
practice	the piano
	the violin
	the cello
an acoustic	guitar
an electric	
a bass	

Percussion

1 drums

2 cymbals

3 a tambourine

4 a marimba

5 maracas

Brass

6 a tuba

7 a French horn

8 a trombone

9 a trumpet

10 a bugle

Woodwind

11 a saxophone

12 a flute

13 an oboe

14 a clarinet

15 a bassoon

16 pan pipes

17 a harmonica

String

18 a sitar

19 a bass

20 a cello

21 a violin

22 a guitar

23 a banjo

24 a harp

Keyboard

25 an electric keyboard

26 a piano

27 an organ

28 an accordion

Words in Action

1. Make a list of famous musicians and the instruments they play.

2. Work with a partner. Pretend to play an instrument. Your partner will guess the instrument. Take turns.

Film, TV, and Music

AGENT 009

1

OFFICER BABY

2

THE RAMIREZ FILES

4

Love in Paris

5

STARDATE 2075

6

A CLUE

3

Dragon Story

8

MIDNIGHT

9

COWBOY

7

A FISH Story

11

HISTORY OF THE PYRAMIDS

10

Films / Movies

1 action / adventure

2 comedy

3 mystery / suspense

4 drama

5 romance

6 science fiction

7 western

8 fantasy

9 horror

10 documentary

11 animated

Word Partnerships

an independent a foreign	film
a funny a scary	movie
satellite cable	TV
a TV	station commercial
loud soft	music

TV programs

12 news

13 sitcom

14 cartoon

15 game show

16 soap opera

17 talk show

18 nature program

19 children's program

20 sports

21 reality show

Music

22 pop

23 jazz

24 rock

25 blues

26 R&B / soul

27 hip hop

28 classical

29 country and western

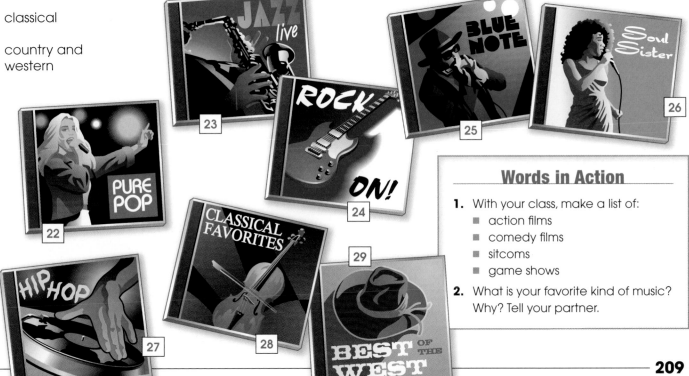

Words in Action

1. With your class, make a list of:
   - action films
   - comedy films
   - sitcoms
   - game shows

2. What is your favorite kind of music? Why? Tell your partner.

Beach

Verbs

30 surf

31 dive

32 swim

33 float

1 a sailboat
2 a pier
3 a water-skier
4 a motorboat
5 the ocean / the water
6 a ship
7 a lighthouse

8 a swimmer
9 a wave
10 a snorkeler
11 a snorkel
12 a sailboard
13 a sailboarder
14 a life jacket
15 a surfer
16 a surfboard

17 a lifeguard
18 a cooler
19 a sunbather
20 a beach ball
21 sand
22 a (sea)shell

23 a water wing
24 sunscreen
25 a sand castle
26 a (diving) mask
27 fins
28 a pail
29 a shovel

Word Partnerships

a public	beach
a private	
a tropical	
a beach	umbrella
	chair
	towel
	house
a bottle of	sunscreen
a tube of	
apply / put on	sunscreen
use	

Words in Action

1. Plan a day at the beach. What will you take to the beach? What will you do there?

2. Think of different ways to group the words in the word list. For example, *Things children play with* or *People and things you see in the water.*

Camping

Word Partnerships

a camping	trip
	site
a fishing	boat
a ski	
a street	map
a city	
a road	

212

1 a compass	8 a canoe	15 a camping stove	22 insect repellent
2 a rock climber	9 a paddle	16 a lantern	23 matches
3 a horseback rider	10 a raft	17 a rope	24 a tent
4 a hiker	11 a backpack	18 a (trail) map	25 a sleeping bag
5 a fishing pole	12 a backpacker	19 a canteen	26 an air mattress
6 a fisherman	13 a water bottle	20 binoculars	27 a camper
7 a (row)boat	14 a (hiking) trail	21 a pocket knife	28 a (camp)fire

Verbs

29 camp

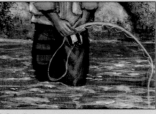

30 fish

31 hike

Words in Action

1. Imagine you are going on a camping trip. What will you do? What will you take?

2. You are lost on a hiking trail. You can only bring five of the items on the list. Which items will you bring? Explain why you need each one.

213

City Park

Words in Context

Central Park is a beautiful **park** in the middle of New York City. It is about two miles* long and has something for everyone. For adults, there are bicycle and jogging paths. For children, there is a **playground** with a **sandbox, monkey bars,** and **swings.** There is even an old **carousel,** an ice rink, and a zoo.

*3.218 kilometers

1 a kite
2 swings
3 monkey bars
4 a playground
5 a slide
6 a jungle gym
7 a seesaw
8 a sandbox
9 a trash can / a garbage can
10 a puppet show
11 a picnic
12 a picnic basket
13 a picnic table
14 a carousel / a merry-go-round
15 a Ferris wheel
16 a roller coaster
17 a bridge
18 a (park) bench

19 a pond
20 a jogger
21 a skateboard
22 a skateboarder
23 a skater
24 (in-line) skates
25 a cyclist
26 a bicycle / a bike
27 a path
28 a street vendor
29 a pigeon

Word Partnerships

a local	park
a national	
an amusement	
ride	a bike
	a carousel
have	a picnic
go on	
fly	a kite

14

15

16

17

18

19

20

21

22

23

24

25

26

27

28

29

Words in Action

1. Work with your class. Discuss your dream park. Draw a picture of the park on the board. Each student adds an item to the park and labels this item.

2. When did you last go to a park? What did you do? What did you see? Tell a partner.

Places to Visit

Words in Context

Try a new activity this weekend. Do you like shopping? You could go to a flea market or a **garage sale.** Do you enjoy nature? You could walk on a **hiking trail** or ride your bicycle on a **bicycle path.** Do you like animals? You could go to a **zoo** or an **aquarium.**

1 a café
2 a zoo
3 a planetarium
4 a nursery
5 a bowling alley
6 a sporting event
7 a pool hall
8 an aquarium
9 a garage sale
10 an amusement park
11 a (hiking) trail
12 a lecture

13 a botanical garden
14 a gym
15 a circus
16 miniature golf
17 a bicycle path
18 a video arcade
19 a carnival
20 a museum
21 a water park
22 a movie theater
23 a rodeo

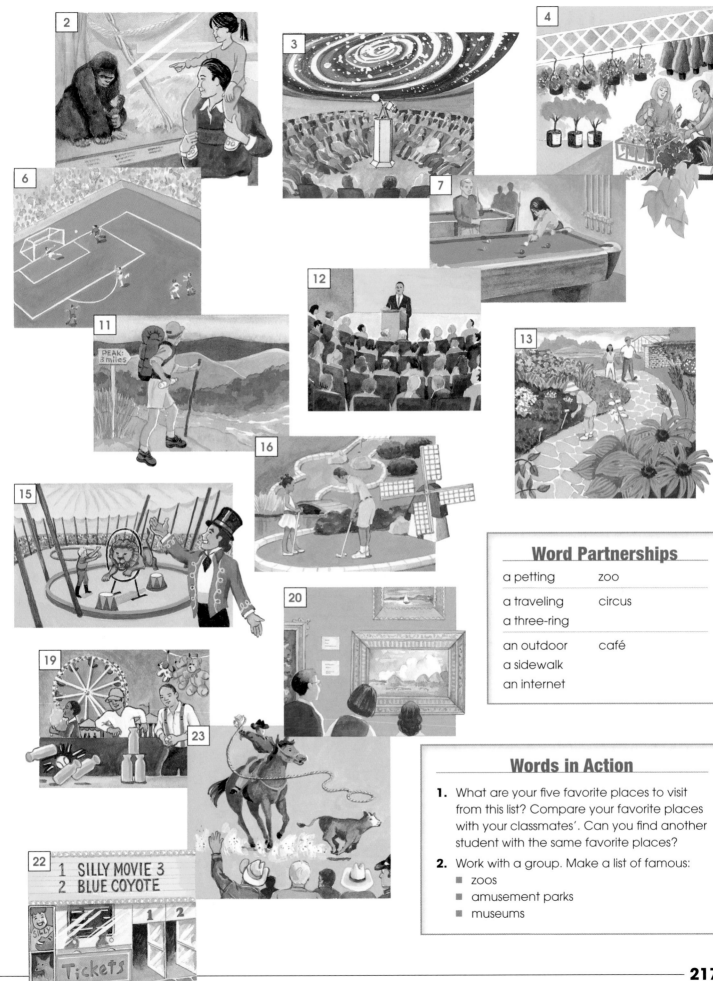

Words in Action

1. What are your five favorite places to visit from this list? Compare your favorite places with your classmates'. Can you find another student with the same favorite places?

2. Work with a group. Make a list of famous:
   - zoos
   - amusement parks
   - museums

Indoor Sports and Fitness

Words in Context

Different sports and fitness activities help in different ways. **Yoga** and **martial arts** can help you relax. **Aerobics** and the **treadmill** can help you lose weight. **Push-ups** and free weights can help you become stronger.

1   martial arts
2   yoga
3   basketball
4   a referee
5   a basketball court
6   a (basketball) player
7   a basketball
8   ping-pong
9   a ping-pong paddle
10 a ping-pong table
11 a chin-up
12 a push-up
13 a sit-up
14 a (stationary) bike
15 a treadmill
16 boxing
17 a boxer
18 a boxing glove
19 a boxing ring
20 a punching bag

21 wrestling
22 a wrestler
23 gymnastics
24 a gymnast
25 weightlifting
26 a weightlifter
27 a bench
28 a barbell
29 a dartboard
30 darts
31 aerobics
32 a diving board
33 a diver
34 a (swimming) pool
35 a locker room

Word Partnerships

sports	club
	team
	equipment
	injury

a yoga	instructor
an aerobics	class
a martial arts	

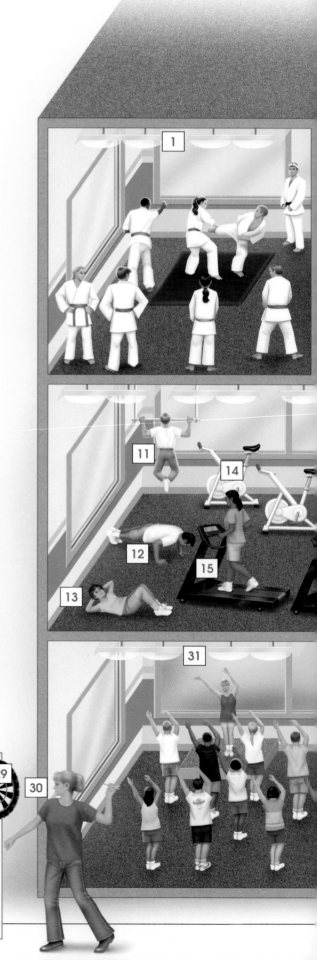

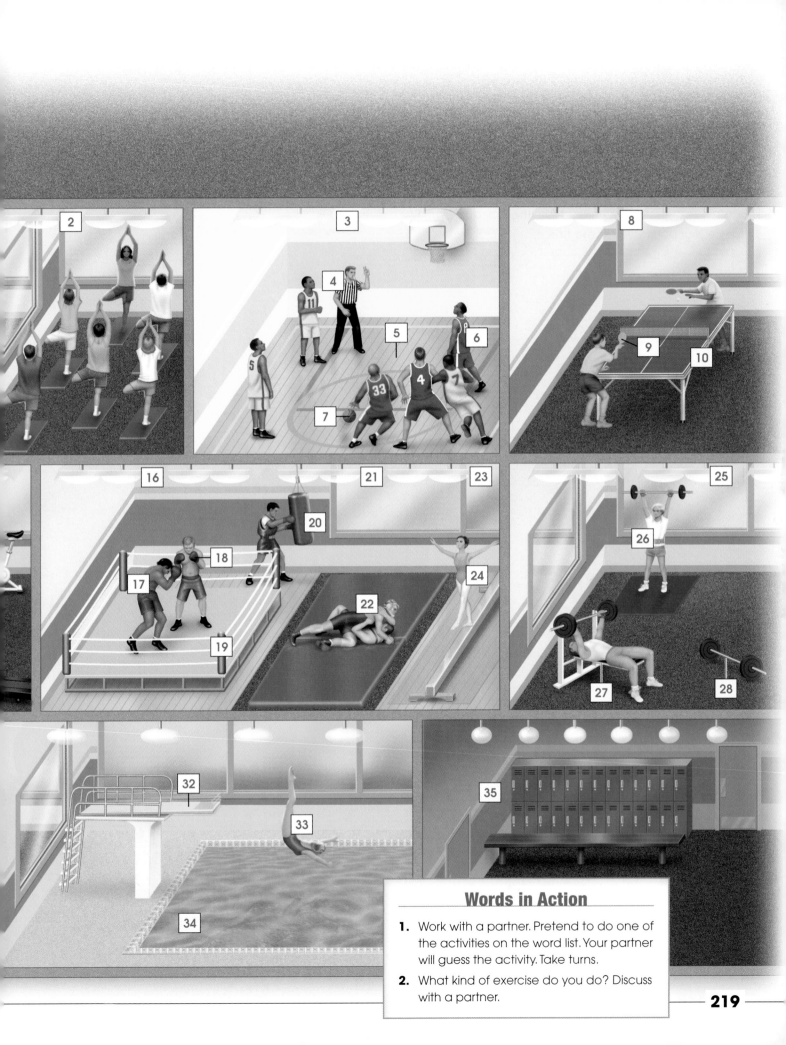

Words in Action

1. Work with a partner. Pretend to do one of the activities on the word list. Your partner will guess the activity. Take turns.

2. What kind of exercise do you do? Discuss with a partner.

Outdoor Sports and Fitness

Words in Context

Tennis is one of the most popular **sports** in the world. The rules are simple. A **player** uses a **racket** to hit a **tennis ball** over the **net.** The other player tries to hit the ball back. The first player to win four points wins the game.

1 tennis

2 a (tennis) racket

3 a (tennis) ball

4 baseball	10 a volleyball	16 track	22 a uniform
5 a baseball	11 a (volleyball) net	17 a runner	23 football
6 a batter	12 golf	18 a track	24 a goalpost
7 a bat	13 a (golf) club	19 soccer	25 a (football) helmet
8 a catcher	14 a golfer	20 a fan	26 a cheerleader
9 volleyball	15 a golf course	21 a soccer field	27 a football

Word Partnerships

a baseball	player
a soccer	
a volleyball	
a rugby	
a golf	ball
a soccer	
a rugby	
hit	the ball
throw	
catch	
kick	
a baseball	glove

Words in Action

1. Which of these sports do you like to play? Which do you like to watch? Discuss with a partner.

2. Work with a partner. One person pretends to play one of these sports. The other guesses the sport. Take turns.

221

Winter Sports

1 a snowmobile	6 ski poles	11 (cross-country) skiing
2 snowshoes	7 a toboggan	12 (downhill) skiing
3 a sled	8 a chairlift	13 a skier
4 skis	9 ice skating	14 snowboarding
5 ski boots	10 an ice skater	15 a snowboarder

16 a snowboard

17 (ice) hockey

18 a scoreboard

19 a score

20 an ice (skating) rink

21 a goal

22 a (hockey) player

23 a hockey stick

24 a (hockey) puck

25 (ice) skates

Words in Action

1. Which winter sports are the most fun? Which are the most dangerous? Discuss with your class.

2. One student names a winter sport. The other students take turns naming clothing and equipment for that sport.
   - Student A: *Hockey.*
   - Student B: *Ice skates.*
   - Student C: *A hockey stick.*

Games, Toys, and Hobbies

Words in Context

Playing **cards** are popular in countries around the world. The French style deck is the most common. This deck has 52 cards and four suits—**spades, hearts, diamonds,** and **clubs.** There are 13 cards in each suit: **ace, king, queen, jack,** and numbers 2 through 10. People use these cards to play different **games** around the world, like *bridge* and *gin rummy* in the U.S., *king* in Brazil, and *dai hin min* in Japan.

1

7   8   9   10

2   3   4   5   6

13 mah-jongg

1 cards

2 an ace

3 a king

4 a queen

5 a jack

6 a joker

7 a spade

8 a diamond

9 a club

10 a heart

11 backgammon

12 chess

14 dominoes

15 checkers

16 a puzzle

17 dice

18 crayons

19 a doll

20 knitting needles

21 yarn

22 a crochet hook

23 (embroidery) thread

24 a needle

Verbs

25 knit

26 crochet

27 embroider

28 build a model

22

21

20

Word Partnerships

a board	game
a card	
a chess	board
a checker	piece
a deck of	cards
a hand of	
play	cards
	a game
king of	hearts
nine of	spades

Words in Action

1. Make a list of your three favorite games from the list. Put the list in order, with the game you like best at the top. Share your list with a partner.

2. Take a poll to find out the favorite games of the students in your class.
   - Which is the most popular game?
   - Which is the least popular game?

Camera, Stereo, and DVD

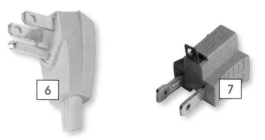

1 (a roll of) film

2 a zoom lens

3 a camera

4 a camcorder

5 a tripod

6 a plug

7 an adapter (plug)

8 a record

9 an MP3 player

10 a (personal) CD player

11 headphones

12 a CD player

13 a CD / a compact disc

14 a speaker

15 a stereo (system)

16 a tape / a cassette

17 a boom box

18 a satellite dish

19 a television / a TV

20 a (video) game system

21 a VCR / a videocassette recorder

22 a video(cassette)

23 a remote control

24 a DVD player

25 a DVD

Word Partnerships

a digital	camera
a 35-millimeter	
a disposable	
shoot	(a roll of) film
develop	
turn up	the TV
turn down	the stereo

Verbs

26 play

27 fast forward

28 rewind

29 pause

30 stop

31 eject

Words in Action

1. Which three items on the list would you most like to get as gifts? Why? Discuss with a partner.

2. Which items on the list could help you learn English? How? Discuss with your class.

Holidays and Celebrations

Words in Context

People celebrate the **New Year** in different ways around the world. In Brazil, many people have **parties.** They often go to the beach after midnight and watch **fireworks.** It is also traditional to throw **flowers** into the sea. The Chinese New Year happens between January 17 and February 19. Chinese people all over the world celebrate with **parades** and **firecrackers.**

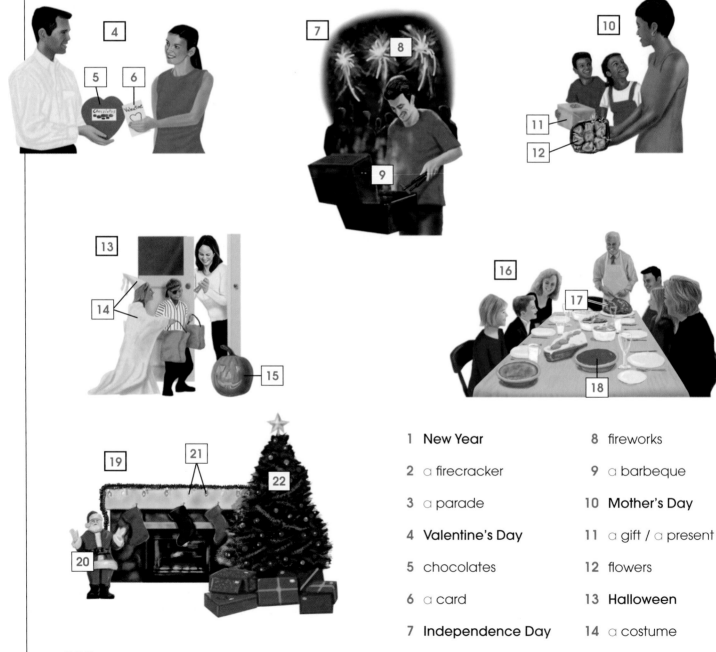

1 **New Year**	8 fireworks
2 a firecracker	9 a barbeque
3 a parade	10 **Mother's Day**
4 **Valentine's Day**	11 a gift / a present
5 chocolates	12 flowers
6 a card	13 **Halloween**
7 **Independence Day**	14 a costume

Verbs

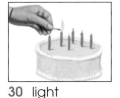

29 wrap
a present

30 light
candles

31 blow out
candles

32 open
a present

3

23

24

25

26

27

28

Word Partnerships

a birthday	party
a retirement	
a New Year's Eve	
a birthday	gift
a wedding	cake
a birthday	card
a Valentine's Day	
a Mother's Day	

15 a jack-o-lantern

16 **Thanksgiving**

17 a turkey

18 a pumpkin pie

19 **Christmas**

20 Santa Claus

21 lights

22 a (Christmas) tree

23 a **birthday**

24 a balloon

25 a cake

26 an **anniversary**

27 a **baby shower**

28 a **retirement**

Words in Action

1. Work with a group. Choose a holiday on the list. What are the different ways the people in your group celebrate this holiday? Discuss with your group.

2. Plan a birthday party for a friend.
- What will you eat?
- How will you decorate?
- What gift will you give?

Index

Index Guide

All entries in the index are followed by a phonetic listing. Following the phonetic listing, most entries have two numbers. The first number, in bold type, is the page number on which the entry item is found. The second number corresponds to the item's number in the word list. See the example below.

Some entries have two numbers in bold type. In this case, the entry is a topic covered in a two-page lesson, and the numbers indicate the page numbers of this lesson.

If the entry is in capital letters, it is a unit title, and the two numbers in bold type indicate the pages on which this unit begins and ends.

If an entry is followed by only a single number in bold type, then the entry appears on this page number as a subhead in the word list, or it appears somewhere else on the page.

Verb and verb phrase entries appear in bold type in the index. Some entries appear twice in the index—once in bold and once in regular type. In these cases, the bold type entry is a verb, and the regular type entry is a noun.

Guide to Pronunciation Symbols

Vowels				Consonants		
Symbol	Key Word	Pronunciation		Symbol	Key Word	Pronunciation
/ɑ/	hot	/hɑt/		/b/	boy	/bɔɪ/
	far	/fɑr/		/d/	day	/deɪ/
/æ/	cat	/kæt/		/ʤ/	just	/ʤʌst/
/aɪ/	fine	/faɪn/		/f/	face	/feɪs/
/aʊ/	house	/haʊs/		/g/	get	/gɛt/
/ɛ/	bed	/bɛd/		/h/	hat	/hæt/
/eɪ/	name	/neɪm/		/k/	car	/kɑr/
/i/	need	/nid/		/l/	light	/laɪt/
/ɪ/	sit	/sɪt/		/m/	my	/maɪ/
/oʊ/	go	/goʊ/		/n/	nine	/naɪn/
/ʊ/	book	/bʊk/		/ŋ/	sing	/sɪŋ/
/u/	boot	/but/		/p/	pen	/pɛn/
/ɔ/	dog	/dɔg/		/r/	right	/raɪt/
	four	/fɔr/		/s/	see	/si/
/ɔɪ/	toy	/tɔɪ/		/t/	tea	/ti/
/ʌ/	cup	/kʌp/		/ʧ/	cheap	/ʧip/
/ɛr/	bird	/bɛrd/		/v/	vote	/voʊt/
/ə/	about	/əˈbaʊt/		/w/	west	/wɛst/
	after	/ˈæftər/		/y/	yes	/yɛs/
				/z/	zoo	/zu/
				/ð/	they	/ðeɪ/
				/θ/	think	/θɪŋk/
				/ʃ/	shoe	/ʃu/
				/ʒ/	vision	/ˈvɪʒən/

Stress

/ˈ/	city	/ˈsɪti/	used before a syllable to show primary (main) stress

hair dryer /hɛr ˈdraɪər/ **144**–6
hair gel /hɛr ʤɛl/ **144**–4
hairnet /ˈhɛrˌnɛt/ **157**–20
hair salon /hɛr səˈlɑn/ **48**–11
hairspray /ˈhɛrˌspreɪ/ **144**–1
hairstylist /ˈhɛrˌstaɪlɪst/ **146**–5
half /hæf/ **3**
half dollar /hæf ˈdɑlər/ **8**–5
half past six /hæf pæst sɪks/ **5**
half sister /hæf sɪstər/ **27**–13
halibut /ˈhæləbət/ **189**–30
Halloween /ˌhæləˈwin/ **228**–13
hallway /ˈhɔlˌweɪ/ **67**–12
ham /hæm/ **87**–4
hamburger /ˈhæmˌbərgər/ **90**–4
hammer /ˈhæmər/ **165**–9
hammer /ˈhæmər/ **160**–9
hammock /ˈhæmək/ **69**–7
hand /hænd/ **133**–4
    raise your... /reɪz yər/ **20**–1
handbag /ˈhændˌbæg/ **109**–2
hand cream /hænd krim/
    tube of... /tub ʌv/ **97**–9
handcuffs /ˈhændˌkʌfs/ **61**–19
handheld (computer) /ˈhændˌhɛld (kəmˈpyutər)/ **25**–16
handicapped parking space /ˈhændiˌkæpt parkɪŋ speɪs/ **58**–14
hand in /hænd ɪn/
    ...your paper /yər ˈpeɪpər/ **20**–2
hand mixer /hænd ˈmɪksər/ **95**–19
hand out /hænd aʊt/
    ...papers /ˈpeɪpərz/ **21**–18
handsaw /ˈhændˌsɔ/ **160**–6
hand tools /hænd tulz/ **160**
hand truck /hænd trʌk/ **157**–19
handyman /ˈhændiˌmæn/ **77**–17
hang /hæŋ/ **183**–28
hang (up) /hæŋ (ʌp)/ **115**–24
hanger /ˈhæŋər/ **117**–11
hang up /hæŋ ʌp/
    ...the phone /ðə foʊn/ **17**–29
happy /ˈhæpi/ **38**–2
hard /hard/ **14**–9
hardcover (book) /ˈhardˌkʌvər (bʊk)/ **55**–13
hard hat /hard hæt/ **156**–8
hardware /ˈhardˌwɛr/ **163**
harmonica /harˈmɑnɪkə/ **207**–17
harp /harp/ **207**–24
hat /hæt/ **104**–17
    hard... /hard/ **156**–8
    knit... /nɪt/ **109**–26
have /hæv/
    ...a conversation /ə ˌkɑnvərˈseɪʃən/ **17**–28, **40**–6
    ...a flat tire /ə flæt taɪr/ **123**–21
    ...a heart attack /ə hart əˈtæk/ **136**–13
    ...an accident /ən ˈæksədənt/ **123**–19
    ...an allergic reaction /ən əˈlɜrdʒɪk riˈækʃən/ **136**–12
    ...breakfast /ˈbrɛkfəst/ **34**–9
    ...dinner /ˈdɪnər/ **34**–19
    ...lunch /lʌnʧ/ **34**–13
have a baby /hæv ə ˈbeɪbi/ **31**–15
hawk /hɔk/ **181**–1
hay /heɪ/ **152**–13
hazardous waste /ˈhæzərdəs weɪst/ **171**–18
head /hɛd/ **133**–19
headache /ˈhɛdˌeɪk/ **135**–13
headlight /ˈhɛdˌlaɪt/ **121**–37
headlights /ˈhɛdˌlaɪts/
    turn on the... /tɜrn ɑn ði/ **123**–7
headline /ˈhɛdˌlaɪn/ **55**–18
headphones /ˈhɛdˌfoʊnz/ **226**–11

put on your... /pʊt ɑn yər/ **126**–16
headset /ˈhɛdˌsɛt/ **16**–16
healing /ˈhilɪŋ/ **136**–137
HEALTH /hɛlθ/ **132**–145
health aide /hɛlθ eɪd/ **146**–21
health club /hɛlθ klʌb/ **48**–13
hear /hɪr/ **17**–26
heart /hart/ **133**–26, **224**–10
heart attack /hart əˈtæk/
    have a... /hæv ə/ **136**–13
heater /ˈhitər/ **121**–20
    ...doesn't work /ˈdʌzənt wɜrk/ **77**–7
heating pad /ˈhitɪŋ pæd/ **142**–21
heavy /ˈhɛvi/ **14**–23, **15**–25
    ...jacket /ˈʤækɪt/ **111**–2
hedge clippers /hɛʤ ˈklɪpərz/ **69**–25
heel /hil/ **133**–17
    high... /haɪ/ **109**–17
heels /hilz/
    high... /haɪ/ **111**–22
    low... /loʊ/ **111**–23
height /haɪt/ **193**
helicopter /ˈhɛliˌkɑptər/ **125**–12
helmet /ˈhɛlmɪt/
    football... /ˈfʊtˌbɔl/ **220**–25
help /hɛlp/ **29**–16, **40**–19
hem /hɛm/ **117**–18
high /haɪ/
    ...heels /hilz/ **111**–22
high chair /haɪ ʧɛr/ **57**–18, **101**–17
high heel /haɪ hil/ **109**–17
high rise (building) /haɪ raɪz (ˈbɪldɪŋ)/ **47**–22
high school /haɪ skul/
    graduate from... /ˈgræʤuˌeɪt frəm/ **31**–5
high school diploma /haɪ skul dɪˈploʊmə/ **43**–28
highway /ˈhaɪˌweɪ/
    get off the... /gɛt ɔf ðə/ **123**–9
    get on the... /gɛt ɑn ðə/ **123**–12
hike /haɪk/ **213**–31
hiker /ˈhaɪkər/ **213**–4
hiking boot /ˈhaɪkɪŋ bʊt/ **109**–24
hiking trail /ˈhaɪkɪŋ treɪl/ **213**–14, **216**–11
hill /hɪl/ **169**–22
hinge /hɪnʤ/ **163**–25
hip /hɪp/ **133**–12
hip hop /hɪp hɑp/ **209**–27
hippopotamus /ˌhɪpəˈpɑtəməs/ **185**–7
hire /haɪr/ **150**–13
hobbies /ˈhɑbiz/ **224**–225
hockey /ˈhɑki/
    ice... /aɪs/ **223**–17
hockey player /ˈhɑki ˈpleɪər/ **223**–22
hockey puck /ˈhɑki pʌk/ **223**–24
hockey stick /ˈhɑki stɪk/ **223**–23
hold /hoʊld/ **29**–4
hole /hoʊl/
    drill a... /drɪl ə/ **165**–4
hole punch /hoʊl pʌnʧ/ **155**–30
holidays /ˈhɑləˌdeɪz/ **228**–229
home /hoʊm/
    go... /goʊ/ **34**–14
home attendant /hoʊm əˈtɛndənt/ **146**–21
home health aide /hoʊm hɛlθ eɪd/ **146**–21
homemaker /ˈhoʊmˌmeɪkər/ **146**–13
homesick /ˈhoʊmˌsɪk/ **39**–16
homework /ˈhoʊmˌwɜrk/
    do... /du/ **34**–17
homework assignment /ˈhoʊmˌwɜrk əˈsaɪnmənt/ **19**–5
honey /ˈhʌni/
    jar of... /ʤar ʌv/ **97**–24

muffin /ˈmʌfɪn/ **90**–14
mug /mʌg/ **70**–30
mugging /ˈmʌgɪŋ/ **61**–9
multiplication /ˌmʌltəpləˈkeɪʃən/ **193**–28
multiplied by /ˈmʌltəˌplaɪd baɪ/ **193**–5
mumps /mʌmps/ **135**–7
mural /ˈmyʊrəl/ **203**–15
murder /ˈmɜrdər/ **61**–10
muscle /ˈmʌsəl/ **133**–2
museum /myuˈziəm/ **59**–24, **216**–20
mushroom /ˈmʌʃˌrum/ **85**–32
music /ˈmyuzɪk/ **209**
    listen to... /ˈlɪsən tə/ **126**–17
musician /myuˈzɪʃən/ **148**–24
music store /ˈmyuzɪk stɔr/ **48**–10
mussel /ˈmʌsəl/ **189**–27
mussels /ˈmʌsəlz/ **87**–17
mustache /ˈmʌˌstæʃ/ **33**–8
mustard /ˈmʌstərd/ **90**–17
mystery /ˈmɪstəri/ **208**–3
nail /neɪl/ **163**–20
    hammer a... /ˈhæmər ə/ **165**–9
nail clipper /neɪl ˈklɪpər/ **144**–12
nail polish /neɪl ˈpɑlɪʃ/ **144**–11
nail salon /neɪl səˈlɑn/ **48**–16
name /neɪm/ **43**–1
    spell your... /spɛl yər/ **20**–13
    write your... /raɪt yər/ **20**–6
nap /næp/
    take a... /teɪk ə/ **34**–15
napkin /ˈnæpkɪn/ **70**–31, **101**–22
narrow /ˈnærou/
    ...tie /taɪ/ **111**–9
nasal (decongestant) spray /ˈneɪzəl (ˌdikənˈʤɛstənt) spreɪ/ **142**–12
nationalities /ˌnæʃəˈnælətiz/ **44–45**
natural disasters /ˈnætʃərəl dɪˈzæstərz/ **170–171**
natural gas /ˈnætʃərəl gæs/ **171**–22
nature program /ˈneɪtʃər ˈprouˌgræm/ **209**–18
nauseous /ˈnɔʃəs/ **135**–19
navy (blue) /ˈneɪvi (blu)/ **10**–11
near /nɪr/ **13**–15
neck /nɛk/ **133**–20
necklace /ˈnɛklɪs/ **109**–8
needle /ˈnidl/ **117**–29, **224**–24
negotiate /nɪˈgouʃiˌeɪt/
    ...the price /ðə praɪs/ **65**–20
neighbors /ˈneɪbərz/
    meet the... /mit ðə/ **64**–15
nephew /ˈnɛfyu/ **27**–20
Neptune /ˈnɛptun/ **176**–21
nervous /ˈnɜrvəs/ **38**–6
nest /nɛst/ **190**–3
net /nɛt/ **25**–29
    volleyball... /ˈvɑliˌbɔl/ **220**–11
new /nu/ **15**–31
newborn /ˈnuˌbɔrn/ **56**–31
New England /nu ˈɪŋglænd/ **172**–11
new moon /nu mun/ **177**–29
news /nuz/ **209**–12
newspaper /ˈnuzˌpeɪpər/ **55**–17
newsstand /ˈnuzˌstænd/ **59**–25
New Year /nu yɪr/ **228**–1
next-day mail /nɛkst-deɪ meɪl/ **52**–19
next to /ˈnɛkst tə/ **13**–11
nickel /ˈnɪkəl/ **8**–2
niece /nis/ **27**–19
Nigerian /naɪˈʤɪriən/ **44**–20
night /naɪt/ **5**
nightgown /ˈnaɪtˌgaun/ **107**–14

nightshirt /ˈnaɪtˌʃɜrt/ **107**–12
night table /naɪt ˈteɪbəl/ **74**–10
nine /naɪn/ **2**
911 /naɪn wʌn wʌn/ **16**–5
nineteen /ˌnaɪnˈtin/ **2**
nineteenth /ˌnaɪnˈtinθ/ **3**
ninety /ˈnaɪnti/ **2**
ninth /naɪnθ/ **3**
nipple /ˈnɪpəl/ **57**–1
noisy /ˈnɔɪzi/ **15**–35
no left turn /nou lɛft tɜrn/ **118**–6
nonfiction section /nanˈfɪkʃən ˈsɛkʃən/ **55**–8
noon /nun/ **5**
north /nɔrθ/ **130**–19
North America /nɔrθ əˈmɛrɪkə/ **174**–8
Northern Canada /ˈnɔrðərn ˈkænədə/ **172**–1
Northern Hemisphere /ˈnɔrðərn ˈhɛməˌsfɪr/ **174**–6
North Pole /nɔrθ poul/ **174**–1
nose /nouz/ **133**–37
    bloody... /ˈblʌdi/ **135**–29
note /nout/
    absence... /ˈæbsəns/ **23**–27
notebook /ˈnoutbuk/ **19**–27
notebook (computer) /ˈnoutbuk (kəmˈpyutər)/ **25**–23
no U-turn /nou ˈyuˌtɜrn/ **118**–11
novel /ˈnɑvəl/ **55**–20
November /nouˈvɛmbər/ **7**–26
nuclear energy /ˈnukliər ˈɛnərʤi/ **171**–28
number /ˈnʌmbər/
    dial a... /ˈdaɪəl ə/ **17**–25
numbers /ˈnʌmbərz/ **1–2**
nurse /nɜrs/ **29**–2
nurse /nɜrs/ **138**–2, **148**–19
    school... /skul/ **23**–8
nursery /ˈnɜrsəri/ **216**–4
nurses' station /ˈnɜrsɪz ˈsteɪʃən/ **138**–1
nut /nʌt/ **163**–23
    wing... /wɪŋ/ **163**–24
nuts /nʌts/ **82–83**
nylon /ˈnaɪˌlɑn/ **113**–10
nylons /ˈnaɪˌlɑnz/ **107**–5
oak (tree) /ouk (tri)/ **179**–5
oasis /ouˈeɪsɪs/ **181**–15
obey /ouˈbeɪ/ **201**–15
oboe /ˈoubou/ **207**–13
observatory /əbˈzɜrvəˌtɔri/ **176**–8
obstetrician /ˌɑbstəˈtrɪʃən/ **141**–10
ocean /ˈouʃən/ **169**–24, **211**–5
October /ɑkˈtoubər/ **7**–25
octopus /ˈɑktəpəs/ **189**–17
off /ɔf/ **13**–7
offer /ˈɔfər/ **102**–20
offer /ˈɔfər/
    make an... /meɪk ən/ **65**–19
office /ˈɔfɪs/ **154–155**
office assistant /ˈɔfɪs əˈsɪstənt/ **155**–19
office building /ˈɔfɪs ˈbɪldɪŋ/ **47**–15
office manager /ˈɔfɪs ˈmænɪʤər/ **155**–6
oil /ɔɪl/ **171**–23
    check the... /tʃɛk ðə/ **123**–16
oil gauge /ɔɪl geɪʤ/ **121**–13
oil spill /ɔɪl spɪl/ **171**–15
old /ould/ **14**–21, **15**–32
olive green /ˈɑlɪv grin/ **10**–6
olive oil /ˈɑlɪv ɔɪl/
    bottle of... /ˈbɑtl ʌv/ **97**–7
    measure... /ˈmɛʒər/ **92**–1
olives /ˈɑlɪvz/ **83**–23
on /ɑn/ **13**–3
one /wʌn/ **2**